THE THIRD WORLD

THE
THIRD
WORLD

THE UNALIGNED COUNTRIES
AND THE WORLD REVOLUTION

By Mario Rossi

FUNK & WAGNALLS COMPANY, INC.

NEW YORK

To Lilly

The removing of those things
that are shaken, as of things
that are made, that those things
which cannot be shaken may remain.

Hebrews 13:28

Acknowledgment

This book is the fruit of literally thousands of interviews with Third World leaders and representatives at the United Nations over the past ten years. I was also helped by writers and journalists with a deep knowledge of the area, and by editors of a newspaper particularly dear to me. A number of those who were unsparing in their assistance, and a rich source of information and orientation, have asked to remain unidentified. It would be unfair to mention names and omit theirs. I prefer, therefore, to express my appreciation to all anonymously. They will recognize, I am sure, the sincerity of my sentiments.

M. R.

Contents

The Third World took a place, after World War II, alongside the Western World and the Communist World. It is "Third" not only because the other two preceded it, dominating the scene of history, but also insofar as it possesses a personality of its own, just as the others do. It is not a world waiting to choose which side to join because it has already chosen to be itself.

The Third World brings to the process of history a new dimension and a new urgency, but also a negation of history prior to its becoming a part thereof; a negation of the ideas, intercontinental relations, and political philosophies evolved without the Third World's participation and without reference to its interests.

Because the Third World is so different and its stage of development so much behind that of the other two worlds, its international perspective is also unlike that of the West or the Communist countries. And this produces a gap in understanding.

The ultimate responsibility for the establishment
of a new equilibrium rests with all countries, but
the problems requiring an immediate solution are
with the West. Third World bitterness and resentment are thus balanced against the West's
lasting impact on Asia and Africa. This contradiction results in a mixture of admiration and
hatred which is at the root of so many doubts and
mistrusts.

So long as the Afro-Asians have unsettled problems with the West and suspect its intentions,
they will also have a vested interest in a powerful
Soviet Union.

The very fact that the United Nations is today
more representative than it was has contributed
to the lessening of its political effectiveness because, until a new economic equilibrium in the
world is reached and the emerging social forces
have consolidated their positions, a type of international relations reflecting these changes cannot
take shape.

To make it possible for the Third World to effect
its integration into the world means to accept the
integration of the world. The forces set loose by

the revolution of our time can be diverted only
at the cost of disaster. They point toward unity
and co-operation. There is no alternative if humanity is to survive.

THE THIRD WORLD

1 Introduction

> The Third World took a place, after World War II, alongside the Western World and the Communist World. It is "Third" not only because the other two preceded it, dominating the scene of history, but also insofar as it possesses a personality of its own, just as the others do. It is not a world waiting to choose which side to join because it has already chosen to be itself.

The uncommitted countries are second only to the Communist countries in eliciting strong feelings on the part of the West, the United States in particular. They arouse either strong criticism, often based on "moral" grounds, or uncritical praise. Little has been done, however, to try to understand them and their policies objectively and without preconceived ideas. To international relations they bring problems and attitudes different from those of the West or the Communist countries. Knowledge must precede praise or criticism and also, more important, a constructive policy for the West. This book, it is hoped, will represent a modest contribution to understanding. No pretense is made to stand in judgment or to take sides. The author believes, however, that there cannot be understanding without a will to understand, and that this in turn requires a sympathetic approach.

When George Leigh Mallory, the famous British explorer, was asked why he had undertaken to conquer Mount Everest, he replied simply, "Because it's there." The Third World, with its ideals and prejudices, greatness and miseries, aspirations and phobias, must be viewed dispassionately because it is there. There is no more impelling reason than this.

The Third World comprises the developing[1] nations of Asia and Africa. It took a place, after World War II, alongside the Western World and the Communist World. It is "Third" not only because the other two preceded it, dominating the scene of history, but also insofar as it possesses a personality of its own, just as the others do. It is not a world waiting to choose which side to join because it has already chosen to be itself. Its vision of the future, its needs, its perspectives are different, and these are all incompatible with the idea that the world can be either democratic in the Western sense or Socialist in the Soviet or Chinese sense. To the old alternatives it has added one of its own. If economic underdevelopment was the only criterion, Latin America would belong in the Third World, too. But that continent does not share with Asia and Africa a number of traits which make of them a world apart. Its traditions, language, and religion belong to the West. It may join the Third World in the defense of common interests, but it remains, just the same, an autonomous entity within the Western community of nations.

The Third World comprises peoples and countries in

a stage of transition from dependence to an independence still short of accomplished fact. This situation represents the dominant theme of Third World political and emotional views of international affairs. It sets the tone for a number of attitudes, some of which will be examined in the following pages. In this respect also, Latin America has points of similarity with the Third World. Strongly subjected to foreign economic interests, it had been allowed to play an insignificant role in international affairs. Its efforts to achieve genuine freedom of action may often lead to attitudes similar to those of the Third World. But if the methods at times coincide, the ends do not.

This book will be concerned more with the themes than the variations. Although the latter are present in abundance, they do not detract from the existence of some fundamental approaches. These, too, may at times reflect an aspiration or a mood, for they are part of a trend which manifests itself in a variety of expressions. For example, while the political experience of the United States differs widely from that of France or Sweden, the three countries still belong to the same Western world. In turn, the Communist countries share a fundamental doctrine even though their interpretations may differ and lead to tension, such as that between the Soviet Union and Communist China. Similarly, the countries of the Third World have common problems and common aspirations, which may be manifested or expressed differently. The exceptions serve to confirm the rule rather than to deny it. The search for regional unity or co-operation in various parts of Asia, Africa, and Latin America in no way contradicts the existence of a Third World, any more than the effort by a number of

Western European countries to join in a European Economic Community contradicts the existence of a Western world.

When the Third World became conscious of its existence, it represented little more than a geographical expression. The only qualification for participating in the Bandung Conference of 1955 was that a country should be located in Asia or Africa. All successive conferences have been either regional or of countries sharing a policy of nonalignment. The existence of an Afro-Asian group at the United Nations, however, indicates that there are common problems and that an effort is being made to find joint solutions. A number of delegates in the group represent governments which are not unaligned, being tied to the West (or in the case of Mongolia to the Soviet Union) by economic, political, or military considerations. These governments share the attitude of the others toward such problems as colonialism, racism, or economic development. They may join the West in a showdown on a specific cold-war issue, but usually follow the rest of their group in problems, such as disarmament, that affect us all.

The Third World is varied and complex, and some of its political attitudes may not be shared by the government of this or that country. These attitudes, however, are sufficiently representative to justify a generalization. Few of the countries allied militarily with the West are democratic enough to allow free expression of public sentiment. While there is evidence that the ideas shared by a majority of the Third World find support, it is difficult to establish to what extent. On the other hand, the number of countries that broke or loosened their ties with the West in order to follow an independent policy has continued to increase over the years. Today they are in the majority. During the same period, very few new nations have reversed a policy of independence in order to enter into binding commitments with foreign powers. The trend is away from such action. For these reasons, when reference is made to Third World attitudes or aims, it must be understood to mean "except for the exceptions." It is important to remember that the countries that do not at the moment follow the general trend also belong to the Third World and share most of its basic aspirations.

The Third World's international outlook reflects the aspirations and convictions of a politically active minority, speaking in behalf of peoples with little knowledge of politics. The masses of Asia living in their desolate villages and the Africans in their tribes have hardly been awakened to the historical changes that have swept humanity. Life for them still goes on in numberless little worlds, distant and unconnected. The leaders of Asia and Africa are engaged in the awesome effort to transform these masses, to mold them to the new ideals. This makes the leaders, in varying degrees, autocratic rulers who must be judged primarily according to their purposes. Even so, they speak for their countries, and the role their countries play in the world depends on the intentions and will of these men. The fact that during the nineteenth century the movement for the unification of Italy was the work of a minority, acting amid the indifference of the masses, indicates how effective such action can be. The same applies to the revolutionary movements in France and other parts of Europe.

For the time being, and until the masses have been awakened politically, Asia and Africa will be identified with their politically and intellectually alert minorities. The two emerging continents will, of course, undergo deep changes, just as the other continents have changed during the last half-century. But certain fundamental trends will remain because they respond to the personality of Asia and Africa. As these continents evolve, so will the others, and the resulting interaction will be felt more and more. Because Asians and Africans have joined the community of independent peoples, the world can no longer be the same.

The author has endeavored to explain some of the fundamental trends behind Third World policies and aspirations as he sees and understands them. If at times they are set forth without attribution, it is only to avoid referring at every sentence to Third World sources or leaders.

11 World-Wide Revolution

The Third World brings to the process of history
a new dimension and a new urgency, but also a
negation of history prior to its becoming a part
thereof; a negation of the ideas, intercontinental
relations, and political philosophies evolved without the Third World's participation and without
reference to its interests.

Wars intensify the process of history in direct proportion
to the turmoil they generate. One such intensification,
caused by World War II, proved to be of unparalleled
proportions. Almost overnight, the world woke up to the
realization that a revolution, compounded of several revolutions, was under way. It shook long-established traditions, ways of life, and approaches to world problems; it
produced social phenomena and transformations. It thus
unleashed forces which under the old order had been re-
pressed or had not found a favorable terrain.

Historians and sociologists have compared today's turmoil to the Industrial Revolution which began in the second half of the eighteenth century and the Agricultural
Revolution which took place twenty-five thousand years

9

ago and changed man into a deliberate cultivator of his food supply. Many of them believe that the present revolution dwarfs its predecessors and that its consequences will be even greater. It is impossible to forecast how it will shift the relationship of man to his environment, but judging from the comparatively recent experience of the Industrial Revolution, we can anticipate changes of fantastic proportions.

Up to that period the ways of society had varied little. Changes in styles and customs had not corresponded to what we identify today with material progress. The means of transportation were fundamentally the same during the Roman Empire, the Middle Ages, or the Renaissance; changes in population occurred at a very slow pace; nor had the life of the populations, most of whom were tied to the land, differed much. The French kings did not possess many more material things than the Roman emperors; homes were lighted by oil lamps and heated by the open hearth; the rhythm of life remained largely the same. Even the inventions of the printing press and gunpowder, with the radical changes they caused, did not affect deeply the ways of life of peoples. The Industrial Revolution, on the other hand, brought about far more changes in a few decades than Europe had known during the preceding two thousand years and released forces which, at an accelerated pace, dominate our lives today.

If it is true that the revolution of our time will prove even more far-reaching in its consequences, we can anticipate changes such as have never before occurred in history. This revolution has just begun. The peaceful applications of nuclear and other forms of energy, the desalting of ocean water that may make deserts bloom, the population explosion affecting certain continents more than others, the new explorations and discoveries in outer space that will add a cosmic dimension to man's life—all this and much more will affect radically our view of the world and our relationship to it.

The present revolution has developed, like the revolutions that preceded it, on many levels—human, social, economic, technical, political—each significant not only in itself but also in relation to the others. This revolution is unique in that it is forcing a reluctant universal approach to human problems. The speed of communications has erased distances; the emergence of the Third World has caused every continent to become a participant in the process of history; nuclear energy has endowed certain nations with the capacity to destroy not only this or that city or region but the whole human race; technology has produced an unparalleled equalization within and among countries; for the first time an organization, the United Nations, represents most of the world. As the British historian Arnold Toynbee said, our century "will be chiefly remembered by future generations not as an era of political conflicts or technical inventions, but as an age in which human society dared to think of the welfare of the whole human race as a practical objective." This has been so because of the interweaving of a number of factors—each one affecting and increasing the impact of the others. Together they destroyed the old order. It would be an idle effort to try to establish which was the most significant. Had one or more of them been absent, history would have followed a different direction and our problems would not be the same.

What distinguishes the revolution of our time is not only that it is the result of deep changes, but also that these changes have occurred simultaneously during a very narrow historical span, and are still acting and reacting upon the whole of humanity. Their effect thus becomes cumulative, like the confluence of violent streams upon a placid river. For example, the discovery of atomic energy would have altered the ways of society under any circumstances, but the fact that it took place during World War II, while the old patterns were being shaken, magnified its importance. Similarly, the discovery of nuclear energy acquired an added significance from the fact of coinciding with the international tensions that go under the name of "cold war." The enormous increase in population in recent years represents a phenomenon that will deeply condition the future course of history, and its impact will be intensified by the expansion of medical facilities and the discovery of new methods of combating diseases which in the past decimated entire populations.

Living in a world of such rapid change, we can do little more than attempt to identify the forces that have been set loose upon the world and establish their connection. Without a knowledge of this connection, however approximate and preliminary, we cannot understand the world of today, or the setting in which national and international politics develop. Whatever affects the relations between men affects also the relations between nations and only against this background can we examine the current political phenomena. Unless we take a universal view of them, there is no hope of even approaching an understanding of our time. The present universal revolution is conditioning international attitudes, whether we are willing to admit it or not. The relations between the United States and the Soviet Union, for instance, would have been very different from what they are today had it not been for the discovery of nuclear power, the emergence of the Third World, and other causes not directly related to the ideological conflict between communism and Western democracy.

A similar confluence of factors, universal in nature, has made possible the "revolution of rising expectations" which dominates the lives of the developing countries; it has produced a degree of economic prosperity in North America and Europe such as had not been thought possible only a decade ago; it has shaken the foundations of traditional patterns in Latin America, leading to social problems which may prove of major significance, and to revolutionary convulsions. But to produce all this, technology would not have been enough. The peoples of the developing countries, for example, had first to evolve the kind of mental outlook that would make impossible the acceptance of past conditions. Only because they did so has the prospect of advancement through technology acquired such immediacy in Asia, Africa, and Latin America. The refusal of people to accept a condition of inferiority as inevitable is a significant product of our age, largely prompted by the increasing equalization brought about by industrial progress and the rational exploitation of natural resources. This equalization was, in turn, the result of a slow and difficult evolution in the West to which not only technology, but also new human values, new approaches to social problems, and the spreading of democratic ideas contributed. Under the revolutionary impact that war brought to a climax, the philosophy behind this equalization mushroomed in the developing countries.

Universalization of history made a significant advance when nationalism reached Asia, Africa, and Latin America at the turn of the century. It was speeded up considerably by World War I. Up to that time "world history" represented no more than the history of Europe and its overseas possessions, and of the rivalries of the European states inside the continent and abroad. But with the end of that war Europe ceased to be the center of the world. It was dwarfed by two world powers—the United States and the Soviet Union. As British historian A. J. P. Taylor has said, theirs "was more than a rivalry of power; it was a rivalry of idealisms. Both dreamt of 'One World,' in which the conflict of states had ceased to exist. Universal revolution on the one side and the Fourteen Points on the other presented Utopian programmes for achieving permanent peace." [1] The emergence of the United States and the Soviet Union to world prominence enlarged considerably the geographical area of historical decisions and introduced ideology as a dominant factor in international relations. Ideology had played no role throughout the period in which the status of Asia and Africa was colonial. The very division of the two continents among the European powers during the second half of the nineteenth century had been the product of relations between states in which ideology had no part whatever. The acquisitions were based purely on national interest and "sacred egoism." Parliamentary England, despotic Russia, imperial Austria, or republican France recognized the same principles of foreign conduct, which were very little influenced by their respective forms of government. The idea that a country uses ideologies in the pursuit of its foreign affairs, or employs its power to promote an ideology, is comparatively new.

The process of universalization brought in its wake universal remedies for the world's ills. These remedies did not lie in the *Republic* or the *City of God* of the philosophers, or in the countless Utopias expressing man's recurring dream of a more perfect society. They were instruments of power wielded by countries possessing the military capacity to destroy humanity. On the Age of Universality there thus became superimposed the Age of Ideology. The first represents an irreversible conquest; the second is probably transient, and prepares the way to a new synthesis. The superimposition of the second upon the first is what marks the present political period in history. The world-embracing approach to problems and the several contrasting visions of the world's future and its "salvation" represent the foundations of international relations today. This new experience has been thrust upon us so suddenly, and its novelty still dominates our lives so thoroughly, that conclusions no sooner are reached than they are relegated to the past. Man finds it difficult to follow the world's evolution and to draw up viable rules of conduct. This contributes to the anxiety, sometimes the hopeless feeling, that weighs so heavily on our generation.

Being last to appear upon the scene as a participant in, and not merely a subject of, historical decisions, the Third

World is particularly affected by the two main character-
istics of international relations today. Its adaptations or
reactions to universality and ideology represent the essence
of its international conduct. The emergence of the Third
World has not been the result of a slow process character-
istic of other parts of the world in different historical
circumstances. Under "normal" conditions, it might have
required several generations for the Third World to reach
the outcome that the acceleration produced by World War
II compressed into a few years. If it is true that history is
now universal because the Third World belongs in it, it
is equally true that the conditions that caused history to
become universal have very little to do with Asia, Africa,
and Latin America. It is important not to confuse the
consequences with the causes, because it is this distinction
that is responsible for the Third World's behavior.

With but few exceptions—notably Algeria and Vietnam
—the countries of the Third World have not known the
protracted and bloody struggles, the battles and revolutions, that many of the nations of Europe had to fight in
order to secure their independence. They became free
primarily because they were caught and carried along in
the whirlwind of the revolution of our time. Of course,
there was a degree of inevitability in independence due
to the fact that the administering countries carried with
them the civilization that was the product of their own
industrial revolution. A large number of Third World
nationalist leaders had studied in Europe and absorbed
its civilization and the principles of democracy and egali-
tarianism on which it was founded. To fight the West
they adopted the principles and the methods of the West.

The nationalist movements, involving only a tiny minority of each population, were basing their struggles and claims on Western traditions and not on those evolved in their own countries. The Western powers had no choice but to reflect their image overseas, and in this resided the inner contradiction of colonialism. The nationalists did not want foreign rule, but knew that they could achieve their aim only by adopting the institutions of their rulers. Their response was less to "oppression or neglect than to the widened horizons opened up by progressive colonial governments." [2] Young people studying in British- or French-run schools about constitutional government or the French Revolution learned their lessons only too well. The adoption by Asian and African intellectuals of principles springing from European traditions caused an anti-European reaction for which Europe was indirectly responsible. The revolution of our time, having originated in Europe, could not but engulf the countries dominated by Europe.

The process by which Europe was undermining its own colonial power through the spread of its own institutions might have been protracted through many more generations, especially in Africa, had it not been for the shift in the balance of power caused by World War II. France, Belgium, and the Netherlands had been defeated and subjugated by the Nazi armies. Britain fought on, but its survival was assured by the intervention of the United States and the Soviet Union. The two countries that emerged as the dominant factor in international politics were traditionally anti-colonialist. Closer to Asian experience was the succession of defeats Japan had inflicted upon the Western powers, furnishing the conclusive proof that the white man was not invincible and unbeatable. The impact of these factors was compounded by wartime promises and declarations, such as the Atlantic Charter and the Four Freedoms.

New waves of national pride, an eagerness to cancel the heavy inheritance of the past and to catch up as speedily as possible with the more progressed peoples, swept through the Third World. China, long treated as a semicolonial country, emerged from the war as one of the Big Five. The United States made good its prewar promise to the Philippines, and on July 4, 1946, the new republic was inaugurated amid the ruins of Manila. Europe could no longer hold its sway over Asia. The Indian army and navy had participated in force in the Allied war effort, playing a decisive role in Africa and the Middle East. When the Indian navy mutinied, the British knew that they could hold their empire only by force. But Britain lacked the strength to check the revolutionary drive unleashed by the war and in 1947 relinquished its Indian Empire. India, Pakistan, Ceylon, Burma, and Nepal emerged as independent countries. Most of Asia was now free, and it would be only a question of time before one colonial bastion after another collapsed. The process that began in the postwar years rapidly led to the liberation of 600 million people.

Even so, it was not generally anticipated at the time that Africa would follow the Asian pattern. There was little doubt that Africa, too, would one day become independent, but it was thought that it might take a long time to bring about the transformations that would make it possible for Africans to rule themselves. The revolution spread to Africa because it was irresistible. The European powers abandoned one territory after another not because they lacked the strength to hold them, but because they recognized the relentlessness of the revolutionary process. With the exception of Algeria, Africans did not have to fight for their freedom. Freedom came to them because it was inevitable and it came with a speed that even their leaders had not considered possible only a few years, or months, earlier.

Free Asia and Africa are thus the products of a global convulsion, of forces which, when set in motion, did not include either continent. Although this revolution soon engulfed the rest of the world, the impulse came from one direction only. That helps explain the Third World's eagerness to try by all means at its disposal to gain a measure of control over the merciless process of change which it did not help create. Because a Third World is the result of the revolution of our time, it cannot behave in the same way as the industrialized countries that were its cause. As the product of the radical, often violent transformation of an established order, these Third World countries instinctively realize that even though the causes of revolutions are often identifiable, no one without the gift of prophecy can say where they will lead. It would be futile to forecast what new international order the present revolution will eventually establish, what will be the relations between men and countries, how the lives of future generations will be affected. What will the world be like when the countries of Asia, Africa, and Latin America reach maturity? What new national and international structure will evolve? What new ideologies or political philosophies will reflect and correspond to this reality?

No one knows, and this admission of ignorance deeply conditions the attitudes of the developing countries. The convulsions of our age affect them far, far more than they do the rest of humanity. Many of them do not have a national identity on which to fall back as have the industrialized countries. As independent countries they do not have a long-established history in which to search for a sense of direction or traditional political institutions which might help them to proceed more confidently. They have "adopted" their political structures from the West and have superimposed them upon a society which is far from ready to absorb them.

The Third World has borrowed from the West, and also from Soviet Russia, some systems and some methods of government, but only for use as instruments in the pursuit of its own goals. That is why the Third World brings to the process of history a new dimension and a new urgency, but also a negation of history prior to its becoming a part thereof; a negation of the ideas, intercontinental relations, and political philosophies evolved without the Third World's participation and without reference to its interests. It also brings its own realization of the hopelessness of trying to anticipate the future.

This is not surprising if we remember that the revolutions of the past have led humanity where no one ever dreamed it would go. They have led also to ideological and political consequences not only unpredictable but also often contrary to the intentions of their instigators.

There are many examples in history of transformations

—in the realm of ideas and socio-economic relations—causing a chain reaction of consequences such as could not have been imagined when the events first occurred. When the principle of toleration was adopted in the seventeenth century, after the Wars of Religion had proved fruitless, no one could have foreseen that the same principle would eventually extend to the realm of politics, preparing the ground for the principles of liberty and equality proclaimed by the French Revolution. Nothing, indeed, could have been further from the intention of autocratic princes. Nor could anyone have forecast when the French Revolution exploded that it would lead to so many isms. None of these isms has won permanence, nor is one ever likely to, though each in turn proclaims that it has the one and final answer to world problems. Isms are either mercilessly suppressed if they run counter to the course of history, or they merely prepare the way for a new system.

In today's ideological struggles—as in the religious struggles of the past which they so closely resemble—there are not, and most probably will not be, victors or vanquished. As the distinguished American jurist Learned Hand wrote: "Most of the issues that mankind sets out to settle, it never does settle. They are not solved because they are incapable of solution, properly speaking, being concerned with incommensurables. . . . The opposing parties seldom agree upon a solution; and the dispute fades into the past unsolved, though perhaps it may be renewed as history and fought over again. It disappears because it is replaced by some compromise that, although not wholly acceptable to either side, offers a tolerable substitute for victory." [3]

The Third World is not alone in believing that Judge

Hand's observation may be true also of the problems of our time. It is important to retain this consideration: that great revolutions follow uncharted courses and their final destination is unpredictable. The new nations, being the product of such change, are the first to sense that today's dogmas will soon have faded into the past.

III The Gap

> Because the Third World is so different and its
> stage of development so much behind that of the
> other two worlds, its international perspective is
> also unlike that of the West or the Communist
> countries. And this produces a gap in understand-
> ing.

Today a deep gap separates the Third World from the
other two worlds, producing a marked impact on international relations as they have developed since the end of
World War II. In fact, the gap is compounded of many
gaps. Three of them are proving particularly important:
the gap in historical evolution; the gap in economic and
social conditions; the gap in understanding. The first is
permanent; the other two, it is to be hoped, will one day
be bridged. So long as they exist together, however, each
increases the impact of the others, and their cumulative
effect will be felt more in the future than it is now. Even
barring major disasters, the closing of those gaps that can
be closed is bound to be a slow and painful process. The
present trend points in the contrary direction—toward a
widening of the distances between the rich and the poor

countries. The realization of this fact is indispensable to an understanding of the Third World and of the perspective it has brought to the consideration of world problems.

While a fundamental unity characterizes both the Western and the Communist worlds, its opposite—diversity—characterizes the Third World. Herein lies the essential difference in historical evolution. The unity of the West results from sharing a common heritage. The inhabitants of Europe have had more of a common history than those of any other continent. Climatic conditions required a civilization of essentially the same type. Nearly all languages spoken in Europe are derived from Indo-European. The spread of science and the arts, as well as military conquest and barbaric invasions brought Europeans together. The unity of Europe was prepared for by the diffusion of Greek culture along the Mediterranean coast, the establishment of Roman domination, and the barbarian invasions which destroyed the social and political organization of the empire. The diffusion of Christianity introduced the same ceremonies, the same moral laws, and the same religious books throughout Europe, where Latin remained for many centuries the language of culture. These traditions were transplanted to America. The divisions within Christianity did not detract from a common faith in the same God and the religious and moral experience of the Gospels. Philosophical traditions in all their varieties have their roots in Greece. The juridical systems draw from the principles of Roman law and their successive interpretations and adaptations to social change.

Unity existed in fact during the Middle Ages when the frontiers of the empire coincided with those of Christianity. In the centuries that followed, it found expression in the autonomy of Western culture. Europe retained a cultural unity based on a common intellectual tradition and a common allegiance to the classical tradition rather than on a common faith.[1] During the last century, apostles of nationalism such as Giuseppe Mazzini viewed the fulfillment of national aspirations as a United States of Europe. Today, this political aim has inspired the creation of a European Economic Community. The wider union represented by the Atlantic community is also founded, despite its strains and stresses, upon the same political and cultural traditions. The Latin Americans share in this heritage, having in common the religion, European languages, the culture, the legal systems, and the philosophical backgrounds.

From unity sprang the principle of equality. "It has its roots," Barbara Ward, the distinguished British economist and author, wrote, "in two profound traditions of Western society: the Greek view of law and the Judeo-Christian vision of souls all equal in the sight of God. For the Greek, the essence of citizenship, what distinguished the *polis*— the city-state—from the barbarous outside, was that men lived in the Greek city according to laws which they themselves had helped to frame. . . . The other mood of equality is expressed in Christian metaphysics, in the vision of souls standing equal in the sight of God." This equality, "innate, metaphysical, and independent of the vanities of class, race or culture," gave rise to a "dominant position in society of men and groups who have never achieved a political 'breakthrough' in any other civilization." [2] The leaven of equality spread gradually from the highest to the lowest strata. In our time, "it underlies the growth of socialism, the cutting edge of trade union organization, the emancipation of the workers in the wake of the middle classes, the whole concept of the modern welfare state." [3]

The Communist world owes its separate existence to a common ideology. Whether this ideological foundation is the product of free consent or tyrannical imposition is not the issue. In terms of international relations, what counts is that the Communist countries have an identity which they recognize (despite their political differences, they basically have a common attitude toward the other two worlds) and which is recognized outside their sphere. Mainland China, North Korea, and North Vietnam, as well as the countries of East Europe, are part of the Communist world. The Communist countries of Asia do not fully belong to the Third World, having decided, or having been compelled, to choose another identity.

The patterns of history have been profoundly different in Asia and Africa. The two continents have no common ground in the sense that there is a Western tradition and a European culture; no common heritage comparable to Christianity, Greek philosophy, and Roman law in the West; no common political objectives as in the Communist countries. The history of Asia has resulted from the interaction of three different types of civilizations—Indian, Chinese, and Moslem—and the influence of events in Central Asia and, later, of European conquests. The Third World's largest member, India, is a conglomeration of numerous races and peoples speaking a great variety of languages (fourteen have been recognized in the Constitution), but having no national language. Religious diversity is to be found everywhere. Burma, Thailand, and Cambodia are predominantly Buddhist; the Philippines are mainly Roman Catholic; Indonesia and Pakistan are almost entirely Moslem. In Africa, the principal religions are Christianity (as in Ethiopia, Liberia, and Ghana) and Islam (as in North Africa, Mali, and Somalia) while large populations still practice animism. About one-third of the world's three thousand languages are spoken in Africa. Large alien minorities contribute to diversification: Chinese throughout Southeast Asia; peoples of Indian origin in South and East Africa; Levantines in West Africa; Europeans in various parts of the continent.

The countries of Africa are, for the most part, artificial creations of imperialism, cutting across tribal and religious units. Even though the tribe is the foundation of social life and personal allegiance, a number of tribes have been partitioned among several countries. Colonialism was not concerned with the elements of unity—tribal or other— that had evolved throughout the continent. Frontiers were the limits of conquest or of agreements among the powers. They were established with a view to the interests of the administering countries, not of the peoples ruled. The same interests at times also dictated the way independence was granted. The Congo was preserved as a unitary state because Belgium thought that was the best way to hold on to its interests there. The French, on the other hand, preferred to break up their West African empire into several small states to compel them to preserve close links with the former motherland. In fact, few of these states have an economy that is even potentially viable; they could not hope to subsist without French economic and financial support. Nearly all the countries of the Middle East were part of the Ottoman Empire and did not exist, within their present boundaries, until after World War I when the British and the French divided the area between them and established the present boundaries.

Diversity in the Third World was unable to produce the revolution of equality. To quote Barbara Ward again: "There was no concept of equality in traditional society. As one knows from still existing tribal societies, leadership lies with the old men of the tribe. There is no way for the 'young man' to claim equality. . . . When tribal society is left behind, the values supported by the leaders are still conservative. They are fixed by an inviolate upper order. . . . In India the fixedness of the pattern extended to everyone. A man is born to his caste and to no other. The very idea of equality is almost meaningless since you are what you are and you cannot measure yourself against other men who are entirely different by birth and by caste." [4] The political units were either too small or too large (empires with few connections between the cities and the villages). They hampered the rise of a middle class capable of exerting a wide economic influence, and operated in a manner contrary to the formation of national identities.

When speaking of the unity of the industrialized world, and the dynamism and expansionist ideas it has produced, as compared to the diversity of the Third World, we are referring to present-day conditions. The Communist world emerged only a few decades before the Third World. It came into existence when the Bolsheviks took power in

Russia during World War I, and expanded greatly after World War II. This expansion coincided in turn with the coming of Asia and Africa to independence. Western Europe was once as primitive as some of the backward parts of the developing continents are now, and its civilization developed slowly. The West's fundamental unity exists in terms of culture and civilization; it is the heritage of the peoples of Europe and the Americas, even when tyrannical and dictatorial governments try to distort or repress it. It outlasted Hitler and Mussolini; it will outlast Franco and Salazar. There is, of course, a great deal of variety within that unity; but it is not as great and fundamental as the diversity within the Third World.

The gap in historical evolution and internal structures between the Third World and the other two worlds is perhaps the most significant element that the rise of Asia and Africa to freedom has added to the pattern of interstate relations. The Third World has introduced diversity —diversity not only within itself but also in respect to the Western and the Communist countries. This new element gives the Third World its independent existence, and the fact that it has one must be taken into account. For continents with different structures, to accommodate this new reality is a difficult task, rendered even more difficult by the gap in social and economic conditions that tend to drive the developed and the developing countries further apart.

The way population growth affects the two parts of the world contributes to the widening of this gap. Before World War I, the population of the industrialized countries grew faster than that of Asia, Africa, or Latin America. In recent years, due to the spread of medical care and the control of epidemics, the population in the poor countries has been increasing twice as fast as that in the rich countries. "Never before in the history of mankind," a United Nations report stated, "have numbers of the human species multiplied as rapidly as in the present century, nor can it be easily conceived that the peopling of the earth will continue at a similar pace in the century which follows. The present era is unique in that a predominance of men in the earthly environment is being established such as has never existed before." [5]

In the years to come the imbalance in population growth among continents is expected to assume alarming proportions. According to rather conservative estimates, between 1950 and 2000—that is, during the most crucial period in the evolution of the Third World—the population of Africa will grow from 199,000,000 to 517,000,000; that of Asia, excluding the Asiatic part of the USSR, from 1,380,000,000 to 3,870,000,000; that of Latin America from 163,000,000 to 592,000,000. Africa and Latin America are at the moment rather sparsely populated and can stand the increase. It is difficult to imagine, however, how Asia can support a population much greater than the total world population today.[6] Nor is it possible to forecast the impact that population pressures of such magnitude will have on the balance of power in the world. For one thing they might discourage the great powers from disarming for fear their international position might be threatened by the sheer weight of human numbers.

Population explosion has contributed to the widening of another gap—that in economic conditions. In recent

years the richer countries have accelerated their progress
to attain a degree of welfare never before achieved. During
the same period, the progress achieved by the developing
countries has hardly managed to keep pace with the rapidly
increasing number of new mouths that need to be fed.[7]
Food consumption is lower than before World War II,
when it was already the lowest in the world. "The disparity
[between rich and poor countries] in standards of nutrition
is now greater than ever, and the number of human beings
living in conditions of hunger and malnutrition is now
larger than ever before in the history of the world." [8]

In recent years, average per capita income in the developing continents increased at the rate of one dollar per
year—hardly enough to make any difference to the average
man.[9] Poverty is reflected in social conditions. The United
Nations estimates that about one-half the total population
of Africa, Asia, and Latin America is homeless or lives
in unsanitary housing.[10] To make matters worse, it is
estimated that over 200,000,000 new inhabitants will crowd
into the cities of those continents during the next ten years.
Medical services are appallingly inadequate throughout
most of the Third World.[11]

Insufficient income not only hampers progress in im-
proving living standards, but does not supply the savings
needed for increasing capital development. Without investment there can be no economic advance and without
economic advance poverty becomes self-perpetuating. Progress is also predicated upon the mobilization of human
resources. "Educated and trained people are always the
chief, and in the long run, the only agents of development.
The unutilized talents of their people constitute the chief

present waste, and the chief future hope, of the developing countries." [12]

Progress in industrialization is essential to economic development. But industrialization requires an agriculture capable of supporting it. Once again—the gap. In the rich countries, a relatively small proportion of the labor force can supply the total population with food and even create a large unmanageable surplus; in the poor countries, the technology of food production is often little different from that described in the Bible. Even though agriculture engages two-thirds or more of their labor force, it does not succeed in feeding the population adequately.

Agricultural development is also needed to free an increasing number of workers for industry. In order to spur agricultural production while gradually reducing the number of people engaged in it, methods must be improved considerably. This need, in turn, often requires sweeping programs of land reform. In the industrialized countries, the land does not represent an obstacle to economic and social progress, except perhaps in Ireland and some parts of southern Europe. In Asia, Africa, and Latin America, on the other hand, structural reforms are urgently needed. Their realization is hampered not only by the conservatism of the peasants, but also by the lack of adequate social reforms. A persistence of the present situation will lead either to stagnation and lack of progress or to violence and social upheavals.

The Third World has initiated a revolution of rising demands just as the economic gap between the rich countries and the poor countries was getting wider. The problem today is: Can the gap be bridged? Are three-quarters of humanity—as the French ethnologist and Director of

Social Science Studies at the Sorbonne, Germaine Tillion, fears—"on the slippery slope of growing impoverishment" for which the only word she was able to find is "pauperization"? [13] Will the Third World's social discontent become a chronic disease? Answers to these questions belong to the future, but they give an indication of the magnitude of the problem. It is no exaggeration to say that they confront humanity with one of the greatest challenges in history.

Because the two gaps, in historical evolution and in economic and social conditions, have such fateful implications, it is no wonder that they permeate the new countries' attitude toward their own and the world's problems. These countries look forward to the establishment of relations between states where the historical gap will not expose them once again to a condition of dependence. At the national level they strive to evolve social orders, responding to the reality of the situation in each country, that favor and hasten the disappearance of the socio-economic gap. Until the two purposes are realized, the Third World will not feel secure in its independence. But their realization presupposes changes in the attitude of the other two worlds not only toward the new countries but also toward each other. Because the Third World is so different and its stage of development so much behind that of the other two worlds, its international perspective is also unlike that of the West or the Communist countries. And this produces a gap in understanding.

The balance that exists today is a stage in the evolution of the relations between societies and nations located in the temperate zone. It does not take the Third World into account because up to the end of World War II that world did not exist as an independent entity. As a consequence, it is not suited to the formation of viable social and national structures in Asia and Africa. The difference in aspirations must be viewed from this angle. In a very broad sense, man's purpose in life is the same everywhere. The Declaration of Independence refers to certain unalienable rights with which all men are endowed by their Creator. But to secure these rights the forms of governments and the social orders vary according to national or regional conditions, the traditions and beliefs of a people, the stages of their development. Peoples want to improve, to change, if necessary, the order of things to fulfill their humanity. Governments are instruments for the attainment of this end. When we say that the aspirations of Asia and Africa are different from those of Europe and America, therefore, we mean that at this particular moment in history the national and international instruments that the latter continents have evolved are not suited, because of the prevailing political, social, and economic conditions, to the realization of a social order that will enable the Asians and the Africans to develop and prosper. The new countries cannot adopt the political systems of other continents, or their methods of conducting foreign affairs because, if they did so, they would defeat the hope of forming viable social and national structures.

What repercussions the gap—that is, all that separates the developed from the developing countries—will have on the course of human events we cannot today anticipate. Too many revolutionary forces are at play and their interaction is ever changing. The gap's impact on the relations among continents is in itself revolutionary. It has added a new perspective to the interpretation of history and opened new "windows" on the world which take in the same scenery, but from a different angle. The consequences will become more serious in the measure that the Third World, and the rest of the world, realize the implication of the gap. Even today, when the consequences are just beginning to be felt, there is a widespread belief that many long-established ways will change because the Third World exists, and is so different. It is already clear that the new countries have added another dimension to political judgment which is neither the West's nor the Soviet Union's. The West, in its relations with the Third World, is not confronted with the irreconcilability of political objectives that produced the cold war. Between the West and the Third World there is rather a gap of understanding as to priorities and emphasis. The West considers communism a greater evil than the condition of poverty and defenselessness in which the majority of humanity lives; the Soviet domination of Eastern Europe worse than the plight of Angola; the fate of East Germans more reprehensible than racial discrimination and brutalities in the Union of South Africa. The Third World takes the opposite view. Determining which is the greater between the two sets of evils is a matter of perspective which varies according to whether the political problems are close to or far from a nation's direct experience. The problem of Berlin, for example, has represented for the average Asian or African the distant echo of struggles in which he was not directly involved. If he happened to be aware of the problem, he could not inject into its consideration the same passions, historical rancors, and ideological values that brought the

West and the Soviet Union into sharp conflict. He simply could not understand why the two blocs got so aroused.

The gap of understanding, the inability to participate, is equally evident in the West's attitudes toward the Third World. Just as the West decries the lack of support of its position on Germany, the Third World condemns the failure to share its own passions over issues in which it is directly involved. Debates at the United Nations have shown how deeply "irrational" (from a Western point of view) the Pakistani and the Indians become over Kashmir. The Arabs are equally "irrational" concerning Israel and accuse the West of cold-blooded insensitivity. The West appeals for objectivity in dealing with the Kashmir or Palestine questions; the Third World urges objectivity on Germany; each resenting the appeal of the other as evidence of a lack of understanding. Each condemns the other's refusal to share its passions even though the motivations behind these passions could not possibly be shared.

Why this difference of approach? Why this inability to agree on the priority to be assigned to the world's problems? Geographic locations are not the answer. Asia is closer to North America than it is to Western Europe; Africa is closer to Western Europe than it is to North America. Yet, Europe and North America have to a large extent a like attitude toward political and international problems despite the vast breadth of the Atlantic which separates them geographically. The causes are deeper and far more fundamental than geographical distances, which jet planes, space craft, and mass communications have practically annulled. They are frequently attributed to the contrast in economic standards. The implication of this view is that once the Third World overcomes its condition of underdevelopment, there will be no substantial differences between it and the developed countries. At that time, so the reasoning goes, the Third World will be ready to adopt forms of government or patterns of international relations already established by the more advanced countries. The problem then will be to induce the Third World to join the West rather than the Communist nations. The Soviets, who share this line of reasoning, hope that it will join them and not the West.

This approach misses the central point. The contrasts in economic development are immensely important but not paramount. Only a few years ago the Soviet Union was underdeveloped compared with the West, but it is catching up fast. In the seventeenth century, an Egyptian fellah and a French farmer had just about the same standards of living; European civilization and Islamic civilization had reached a comparable stage of development.[14] The economic inequalities among continents go back no more than two or three centuries and have acquired their present proportions only in recent decades. The ratio between the per capita income in India and the United States was 1 to 15 in 1938 but 1 to 35 in 1952. Economic disparities, therefore, are a rather recent phenomenon. They are frighteningly threatening and constitute one of the main factors in international relations today—but even so, they do not tell the whole story.

There are certain aspects of the gap that will exist even when the Third World is poor no more. They represent a rich diversity, the contribution of ancient and honored civilizations that can only enrich the world that has emerged upon the ruins of the last war. If today they contribute instead to the increase of contrasts among nations, it is because of those factors which widen the gap of understanding.

iv Peaceful Coexistence

> Peaceful coexistence is not a policy reflecting tran-
> sient conditions or abstract ideologies, but an ob-
> jective which the Third World can ignore only at
> the peril of its existence as an independent entity.

Upon becoming free from foreign control, the countries
of the Third World entered into diplomatic contact with
states that had refined international relations when colonies were mere instruments of power of the colonizers. Foreign policy up to that time had taken into account only
remotely and indirectly the wishes and aspirations of
Asia and Africa. Its pattern had evolved within the context
of relations between long-established nations whose cen-
tury-old aims included the increase of power. There was
no precedent for intercontinental relations, at least not
of a magnitude such as obtains today. Nations, not continents, dealt with one another, as equals if they were of
like strength, or by imposing their wills when they could.

These traditional rules of conduct could not apply to
the new situation brought about by the rise of Asia and
Africa. For the first time in history a new relationship

39

arose—that of the rich countries and the poor countries. The world's proletarian nations appeared on the scene of history with an impact that only a gigantic revolution could produce, in little over a decade some fifty of them, representing over 1,000,000,000 people. Their mentality and outlook had been shaped during the colonial period and reflect an experience unknown to any other peoples elsewhere. We are often inclined to think of these nations in terms of our Western experience and to consider them no different from what others have been during the early period of their history. The fact is that they are different, profoundly so. They are linked together not by a common heritage or a community of beliefs, but simply by their condition of underdevelopment. As former Prime Minister Mamadou Dia of Senegal wrote: "It is the consciousness of economic inequality that gives birth to a proletarian national sentiment, aligning the nations of Africa and Asia on the same battlefront against the West. With the consciousness of underdevelopment, a new idea appears, that of proletarian nations grouped 'on the lifeline of imperialism' confronting rich nations with a geographical unity that widens the gap between them." [1] The basic division established by the Third World is not along the traditional lines of the relations between states, but a far wider division which sets the rich industrialized countries on the one side and the poor proletarian nations on the other.

This assumption weighs heavily in the Third World's attitudes in the realm of international relations. The gap dividing the countries of Europe (West and East) and

North America from Asia and Africa is a determining factor in influencing all others.

Basically, this new perspective is dictated by the consideration that the new nations lack the fundamental conditions for the effective exercise of sovereignty. Sovereignty, in the Third World, represents the instrument for building a new nation, or consolidating states that, as artificial creations of the imperialist era, do not even possess a national history. The fact that the developing countries are new is not the determining element. All states were new at some moment in their history. But in the past it was assumed, even though it was not always true, that independence was the final act upon reaching viability.

In the Third World, independence preceded viability, so that in a sense the traditional pattern of evolution to nationhood was reversed. A nation cannot be built on the quicksand of insufficiency and dependence. Without a concrete socio-economic base, independence is fragile, often illusory. The developing countries find themselves midstream, well beyond the point of no return, but facing a long, rough, and dangerous voyage. The changes produced by colonialism were deep enough to exclude the return to conditions such as existed before the colonial era, but not sufficiently deep to render the developing countries secure in their independence. They cannot take their independence for granted, not only because it is new and feebly founded, but also because they do not possess, singly or collectively, the power to defend it.

Asia and Africa are still little more than geographical expressions. Their personalities stem from a past that was often glorious, but has little to offer to the modern world. Centuries ago, India and China had a splendidly developed civilization while Europe lived in a state of semibarbarism. Then came a period of decadence from which the two countries never fully recovered. Europe, meanwhile, was preparing the ground for a social, political, and cultural evolution that has continued uninterrupted to this day. In the Third World, decadence paved the way to colonialism; in Europe, to new recoveries. As a consequence, independence has for the developing countries meaning and significance of a nature that the West has outlived and often finds difficult to understand. History, in the memory of Asians and Africans, is their colonial experience, and all the good and bad it has left in their heritage. Beyond that period there is very little historical experience that can help them solve their present problems or give them a sense of direction. The future may be bright and prosperous once viability is reached, but between now and then there will be a long period of decolonization, of transition from one political entity to another.

During this period, the Third World will need the tranquillity to concentrate on its internal problems and the confidence that the task will proceed unhampered. It is finding instead insecurity amid international conditions of unprecedented tensions; and this insecurity has contributed to a complex of fears and responses to fears not less deeply felt because the West often finds them exasperating. The main reason for this trait that marks the Third World's appearance upon the scene of history is that most of Africa and Asia would not be independent today were it not for a number of *external* factors which are beyond their power to control.

The irresistible acceleration produced by converging revolutions that catapulted two continents to freedom was little influenced by the forces at work from within. The stage of preparation for independence made little difference, nor were the stages of economic development considered; colonies were freed one after another, without reference to internal conditions, because a historical evolution beyond the power of governments to control demanded not so much that this or that country be freed, but that the *whole of Asia* and the *whole of Africa* should acquire independence. It was the same urge that produced the political division, also new in history, between developed and underdeveloped countries. This new terminology reflects a new reality that has found a place alongside, and at times in contrast with, the traditional ways of conducting international relations.

The Third World is reluctant to admit that it owes its existence to forces it did not set in motion and consequently cannot steer. But actually it is deeply aware of this reality and of its implications for the future—all the more so because external factors have also contributed to the preservation of its independence. The West holds that the granting of freedom to the former colonies was unconditional and irreversible. It rejects indignantly as cheap propaganda the Soviet contention that only the might of the Communist camp has saved the developing countries from falling again under the heels of "capitalistic imperialism."

By and large, the Third World does not agree with

either view. It is not at all certain that the process of history cannot be reversed and that it cannot fall under a different form of foreign control. Even though the developing countries lack the strength to defend their freedom with their own means, they do not want to be "saved" by the Soviets or by the West. On the contrary, they take advantage of the competition between the two blocs in the hope that they will deter each other from interfering. This helps to explain why the cold war, by providing "another side" to which to turn in case of real or imaginary threats, affords them a relative sense of security. Postwar experience has borne out this thesis a number of times.

Had it not been for fear of Soviet intervention, the United States might not have acted so energetically in 1956 to protect the sovereignty of Egypt following the Anglo-French-Israeli attack on Suez. The same fear probably discouraged some Western powers from intervening in the Congo when serious anti-white violence erupted in the wake of independence in 1960. Fear of Western intervention also deterred the Soviet Union from taking advantage of the confusion in an effort to establish a presence in the central African territory. This mutual neutralization was principally responsible for the intervention of the United Nations which sealed the Congo off from the cold war and enabled the former Belgian colony to preserve its sovereignty. In Southeast Asia the future depends in the last analysis on the great powers, Communist China, the United States, and the Soviet Union. This was shown to be true in Vietnam and Laos. Nothing but fear of seeing the Sino-Soviet bloc extend its influence was responsible for the United States' decision to intervene militarily to preserve the independence of South Korea.

For opposite reasons the two military blocs have an interest in preserving the identity of the developing countries—Washington to protect them from "Communist subversion" and Moscow to save them from "Western imperialism." This situation is largely responsible for the eagerness which Washington and Moscow display in seeking Afro-Asian support at the United Nations and overshadows the fact that the countries of Asia and Africa are numerically the strongest within the organization. In the present tense international situation, the major powers are willing to pay a price to gain the sympathy of other nations, or at least to prevent their competitors from getting it. Under different conditions, the developing countries might not have received economic and technical assistance so lavishly, nor would they have been in a position to threaten to turn to the "other side" in order to get more and more. The same method is often employed to counter political initiatives which Asians and Africans find displeasing or threatening. The Third World fears that its independence would be compromised if it did not have sides to choose as occasions arise.

Dependence, as the word indicates, implies lack of effective equality. It means that a country is not able to stand on its own feet and that if the external conditions that have presided over its independence changed, it would have no means of defending its sovereignty.

The contradictions caused by an excessive dependence upon external factors, and the immense problems they create for the developing countries and the whole world, will not cease until viability is reached. These countries will have little control over their own destinies unless they modernize sufficiently to build a solid base for their independence. They will not be truly free unless their freedom is primarily the result not of external but of *internal* factors, which they are responsible for shaping and which it is in their power to control. A country increases its effective independence to the extent that it reduces the necessity for dependence. The very fact that the Third World must rely upon external factors to survive is in itself a serious indication of dependence.

The paramount problem of the Third World is therefore to achieve a degree of modernization sufficient to ensure receiving equal treatment from the established nations. It is, of course, not necessary for two countries to reach the same degree of development in order to establish a condition of equality, provided the gap that separates them is not unreasonably wide. The Third World can be secure in its independence when the gap that separates it from the industrialized countries is reduced to reasonable proportions. The Third World's first and basic objective of foreign relations is to undertake today whatever initiative it deems conducive to the realization of this end. The means used in the pursuit of this policy may not always be of a nature to win the approval of the West, or often of the Communist countries, but they are being applied to situations such as have never before existed. There is no precedent for two continents acquiring independence so suddenly and subordinating their main foreign policy considerations to the realization of this objective. The world is slowly learning to live with this new experience as it does with other aspects of the revolution of our time. Its consequences will be felt more and more as the Third World progresses.

If the means are unprecedented, the ends are not. In this respect there is little difference between sovereign countries. The West's main purpose today is to preserve its traditions, institutions, and interests from the onslaught of communism. The Soviets' main purpose, at least officially, is to defend and propagate the Communist system. These purposes become identified with the national interest and inspire the perspectives which the West and the Soviet Union bring to the conduct of international relations. The immediate purpose of the Third World is to increase its reliance upon internal factors, and gradually reduce its dependence on external factors, and *that* becomes the perspective which inspires its every international move. And just as the United States judges the initiatives of other countries by whether they are likely to strengthen or weaken their responses to Communist pressures, the Third World judges other countries' iniatives by whether or not they favor its immediate purpose of speeding development.

Development means far more than economic progress. It requires men trained to perform a multiplicity of tasks in the administration, industry, agriculture, and commerce. Training means specialized schools and teachers. Specialized schools require a high level of literacy. All this requires planning that cannot be done without a functioning government. But government requires political institutions and a basic political philosophy to inspire them. In short, the goal of development is a functioning state. In varying degrees every country in Asia and Africa faces the same problems. Each has abandoned its colonial institutions and is striving toward national institutions. During the transition period, through decolonization to viability, the countries of the Third World have to devise or improvise methods to fit their unprecedented situation. Most of them have soon realized that without the continued technical and financial assistance of their former masters, their political and administrative structures would not withstand the shock of independence. The problem has become how to make dependence and independence coexist. Many Third World foreign-policy attitudes are the product of this dilemma.

Improvisations and day-to-day adaptation to new challenges are not sufficient to lead the developing countries through the transition period. There must be a long-range and sustained policy that favors, not hinders, the process of development. This calls for far more than economic and technical assistance. It requires an international climate that will make possible the realization of Third World objectives.

In the past, and to a large extent even today, the centers of policy-making decisions at the international level have not included the developing countries. Indian policy was made in London, North African policy in Paris and Madrid, Congolese policy in Brussels, Indonesian policy at The Hague—in behalf of and for the pursuit of the national interest of Britain, France, Spain, Belgium, or the Netherlands. Today, Indian policy is made in New Delhi; North African policy in Tunis, Rabat, and Algiers; Congolese policy in Leopoldville; Indonesian policy in

Djakarta. It is pursued not in the interest of the colonizers but of the countries immediately concerned.

Yet, despite this new freedom of action, the developing countries are hampered in the fulfillment of their tasks by what they consider an excessive world concern with the interests and the problems of the industrialized countries. So long as the latter continue to be the center of the world, international relations will not take sufficiently into account, and will often be at variance with, the interests and problems of the developing countries. The Third World no longer wishes to live in the shadow of the Western and the Communist worlds. It looks forward to the time when the decision-making process will extend to the whole world and every country within it.

The achievement of this aim would mean that for the first time since the dawn of civilization, history would be truly universal. Of course, universality cannot be achieved so long as the world is pulled in three different directions and subjected to the contrasting philosophies and views of the future that today inspire the West, the Communist countries, and the Third World. Universality can result only from a synthesis capable of submerging the contrasts in the name of a higher goal. The developing countries urge the world in the direction of universality not because they are better or more idealistic than the other countries, but simply because they have no alternative if they are to participate actively in decisions affecting the future of the world, and thus be in a position to protect their own interests and guarantee their own independence. Because they are weak, the impact of their pressures is limited.

The industrialized countries are and will continue to be

for a long time the main initiators of world-affecting decisions, because only they can decide if there shall be peace or war on earth. Their responsibilities are correspondingly great and cannot be surrendered, whether the Third World likes it or not. The balance of terror, despite its frightening implications, is the only guarantee of non-war today.

Because the industrialized countries are so deeply divided into two blocs that neutralize each other, the Third World can exercise an influence and exert pressures that its weakness would otherwise make impossible. But it can do so only if its component parts strive to act in concert, finding in cooperation the strength needed to defend their own views. Cooperation among nations is the result of a series of compromises, of a willingness to subordinate the factors leading to contrast to a higher and more urgent purpose. If the task is difficult for groupings characterized by unity, it is even more so for the Third World because of its diversity. The effects of this diversity were in turn rendered more acute by the past isolation of Asia and Africa.

Throughout the long colonial period there had been no intercourse between the countries of the Third World. Isolation was the result not only of historical conditions but also of a deliberate policy on the part of the administering countries. Colonies were to be "protected" from outside interference and linked with the mother country only. This policy served to insulate them from the ambitions of rival powers and from contacts with influences that would have complicated the task of administration. As a consequence, there was an almost total lack of contact even between the intellectuals in the administered countries. They lived as if in worlds apart, although a few young Asians and Africans would meet in one of the European capitals, if their families had the means to send them there to study. In his autobiography, Nehru recalls his student years in England and the Western and Eastern European countries he visited. There is no mention of visits to countries of Asia and Africa, except for brief stopovers in Cairo.

Nehru's experience has been the same as that of other Third World leaders during the colonial period. President Sukarno of Indonesia stated: "It is a new departure in the history of the world that leaders of Asian and African peoples can meet together in their own countries to discuss and deliberate upon matters of common concern. Only a few decades ago it was frequently necessary to travel to other countries and even other continents before the spokesmen of our peoples could confer. I recall in this connection the Conference of the 'League Against Imperialism and Colonialism' which was held in Brussels [in 1927] . . . But that was a meeting place thousands of miles away, amidst foreign people, in a foreign country, in a foreign continent. It was not assembled there by choice, but by necessity." Isolation had not been a matter of policy, as for a time with the United States and the Soviet Union, but the result of historical conditions.

Because of this lack of communication, the countries of the Third World were strangers to one another when they became independent. While they had a fairly good knowledge of their former masters, they knew next to nothing about their neighbors. Their immediate effort was, therefore, to come to know one another. They first met together at the Bandung Conference of African and Asian states held in 1955. A number of speakers at that historic meeting stressed that its main purpose was precisely to enable the leaders of Africa and Asia to get acquainted and discuss their common problems.

The conference had another important effect. It offered the clearest demonstration of how diverse were the countries representing the Third World. There was no common link of language, religion, race, and historical traditions, but only of negative factors such as a past of colonial domination, an economic condition of underdevelopment, suspicion toward the West, deep racial feelings, and an eagerness to end the condition of inferiority in relation to the rest of the world. This diversity was not offset by a common political and ideological foundation. Consequently, these countries had to establish among themselves the kind of relationship that would enable parliamentary India to live at peace and co-operate with authoritarian Ethiopia, Buddhist Burma with Moslem Pakistan, leftist Indonesia with feudal Saudi Arabia. For a number of countries the need of creating unity out of diversity reflected an internal necessity.

In the circumstances, cooperation was not an easy task, but what else could these countries oppose to the overwhelming military, technical, and financial power of the West and of the Communist bloc except the strength that derives from representing two-thirds of humanity? The realization of this goal required a policy that would enable these most diverse countries to join in the pursuit of common objectives *despite* their different political systems.

That was the beginning of the policy of peaceful coexistence, for which the primary motivation was the composition of the Third World and the inner structure of a number of countries represented therein. This policy, as interpreted by Africans and Asians, has only the name in common with the type of coexistence advocated by the Soviet Union. Peaceful coexistence is not a policy reflecting transient conditions or abstract ideologies, but an objective which the Third World can ignore only at the peril of its existence as an independent entity. It means that countries must learn to live at peace and to cooperate with one another, irrespective of political systems or ideologies. As a consequence, a country's form of government becomes purely an internal matter which cannot be allowed to affect the relations between states. Today's political realities seldom conform to this objective because it does not take into sufficient account the responsibilities that go with the exercise of power.

If the countries of the Third World share no common political and ideological foundation, they have even less in common with the West and the Soviet Union. The problems they face on a regional scale exist also on a world scale and in their view the approach could not be different. If peaceful coexistence was the only valid form of relationship among the Afro-Asian countries, it had to be also the essence of their relationship with the other countries and for the same reason. The powers, however, had become used to managing their foreign relations on an entirely different basis. They champion conflicting ideologies which are intrinsically intolerant, each being dedicated to the destruction of the other's. The problem for the Third World thus became how to cooperate with the West and the Soviet Union despite and irrespective of their ideologies.

The Third World solved this problem by rejecting ideology as an instrument of power. In order to cooperate among themselves, these countries had to show respect, or at least tolerance, toward other ideologies and political philosophies unless they became aggressive. These were to be considered an internal matter and play no role in the relations between states. The same considerations had to apply to countries outside its own area, because the Third World could find no other basis on which to deal with the Western or the Communist countries. Denial of the claims of ideology as an instrument of power in the Age of Ideology has introduced a perspective of great significance. It means first of all that the Third World will dissociate communism from power in the relations with the Soviet Union and democracy from power in the relations with the West.

Western democracy and *Soviet* or *Chinese* communism represent the fruit of historical circumstances which the Third World has not shared. Democracy, as understood in the West, is a by-product of the Industrial Revolution which has bypassed Asia and Africa. The Industrial Revolution came first, modern democracy later. Asia and Africa have not yet had their industrial revolution. Democracy as understood by *them* corresponds to different sets of historical circumstances and present-day conditions.

The same consideration applies to communism. The developing countries have been conditioned by colonialism, an experience that had nothing to do with ideology. Territories overseas were conquered to increase power and not to spread ideologies, and the administering countries made no efforts to impose one on their colonies. The Third World is the result of world-wide revolutionary changes and has developed amidst changes. It cannot see any point in adopting other people's ideologies, such as are being promoted today as instruments of foreign relations, strictly related to particular interests. These ideologies came to maturity in entirely different settings and may be superseded as the world adapts to the age of cosmic discoveries. That does not mean that the *principles* of democracy and socialism are being rejected, but only that particular form of democracy which the West says it defends in its cold war with the Soviet Union, and that particular form of socialism which the Soviet Union and China say they defend in their cold war with the West.

In the Third World's present condition, its primary concern—the achievement of viability—is dictated by practical and contingent considerations. It represents an ideal but certainly not an ideology. Ideological involvement would prevent Third World countries from turning to both East and West for the economic and technical assistance required until they can stand on their own feet. It would also make impossible the playing of one participant in the cold war against the other in order to preserve a condition that today affords the Third World a certain sense of security. The paramount reason for ideological rejection, however, is not tied to transient reasons, such as the current transition from decolonization to independence. Ideologies are divisive and irreconcilable with a world outlook. Consequently, peaceful coexistence cannot be realized except through the rejection of ideologies as instruments of foreign relations.

The implications of this demand would change the pattern of foreign relations. To extend the scope of international relations so that it will embrace the whole world means shifting the center of attention to problems other than ideological. Historical interpretations are related to the peoples, the places, and the moments which generated them. In time and space, history has more than one dimension. The Third World believes that the essential problem of our time is not the conflict of ideologies, but conditions that affect and concern a majority of humanity, such as poverty, illiteracy, racism, hunger, economic insecurity. These, the Third World believes, are the real threats, endangering the peace of humanity because they could lead to a catastrophic confrontation between the poor and the rich nations. Ideologies represent artificial threats, which nations exploit to pursue policies of their own, but which need not divide the world. They are recently forged instruments of political pressures, while the ills affecting a vast majority of humanity have deep causes requiring drastic remedies.

Long before India became independent, Nehru wrote: "The problems that face us are not Asiatic or European problems, but world problems or problems of humanity. And unless we solve them for the whole world, there will continue to be trouble. Such a solution can only mean the ending of poverty and misery everywhere. This may take a long time, but we must aim at this, and nothing less than this. Only then can we have real culture and civilization based on equality, where there is no exploitation of any

country or class. Such a society will be a creative and progressive society, adapting itself to changing circumstances,
and basing itself on the cooperation of its members. And
ultimately it must spread all over the world. There will be
no danger of such a civilization collapsing or decaying, as
the old civilizations did. So while we struggle for the freedom of India, we must remember that the great aim is
human freedom, which includes the freedom of our people
as well as other peoples." [2]

What characterizes our age, from the Third World's
perspective, is the formation of new nations, the effort to
liberate those still under colonial rule, the rapid decline of
empires. Humanity's main task is to overcome the problems created by these new historical forces. Whatever de-
tracts from this essential concern runs counter to the new
directions that history today urges upon the world. The
developing countries often dramatize their inability to side
with either of the two blocs dividing the industrialized
nations, or their aspirations to globalism, by stressing
the Third World's identification with the whole human
race and with the entire world. This theme has run through
speeches and declarations at every Third World conference
and often rings in the United Nations assemblies. It is
stretched at times to the rather presumptuous conclusion
that the Third World represents the "conscience of humanity."

Weak countries often find in abstractions and principles
some compensation for their lack of power. That helps to
explain why the Latin Americans are so passionately concerned with international law, which offers a set of rules
to regulate the relations between states irrespective of

their power, thus in effect guaranteeing their equality. If the industrialized countries recognized the primacy of justice, human solidarity, peace, freedom, and other principles which Third World leaders proclaim—even when they do not always practice them—the disparity in power between the United States and Ghana or between the Soviet Union and Ceylon would not detract from their equality. The Third World cannot become fully "involved in mankinde," as it so ardently wishes to do, so long as its perspective is ignored by the great powers in an effort to extend their ideological influence. Many leaders of developing countries have made it clear that they consider ideological propaganda a form of "subversion of thought," to be placed on a par with other forms of subversion and interference. As Prince Sihanouk of Cambodia stated, peaceful coexistence "must be a renunciation of the idea of conquering the minds of men by propaganda and subversion, or by anything that constitutes a psychological assault and breach of trust." It also "presupposes the refusal to denationalize a country by corruption or indoctrination of one group of citizens to make them abandon the true interests of their fatherland and pay no heed to the profound feelings of their people." This attitude represents the very foundation of the policy of nonalignment with which the Third World has increasingly become identified.

What started as a new dimension deriving from the Third World's inner structure has rapidly evolved into a new perspective that is increasingly influencing the patterns of international relations.

v Anticolonialism

> "Colonialism" refers today far less to colonies than to the process of decolonization, which represents one of the most complex and threatening problems facing humanity.

The Third World's ideal of seeing a condition of parity established between the developed and the developing countries will meet with formidable obstacles. It is based upon the acceptance of a historical interpretation that recognizes in the emergence of Asia and Africa, rather than in the ideological competition dividing the industrialized countries today, the most significant happening of our time. The late United Nations Secretary-General Dag Hammarskjöld shared this view when he declared: "No matter how overwhelming other world problems may appear to us because of their proximity, it is possible the future will attach greater importance to the rebirth of Asia and Africa in the historical evolution of the present epoch than to the questions now uppermost in the news." [1] Hammarskjöld envisioned a world where all countries and nations, rich and poor, old and new, would participate in "the evolution towards the synthesis which is on the way."

The realization of this aim will not just happen. It requires a mental reorientation for which the West and the Communist worlds are not prepared. Nor are the developing countries yet in a position to exert a sufficient degree of pressure to force upon the industrialized countries their view of what is vital and lasting. The established camps are inclined to project into the future a Third World only slightly changed from the present. They would be wiser to anticipate that though the transition from colony to independence has been largely smooth and peaceful, the process of decolonization is bound to be violent. The tremendous effort needed to bridge the gap between the developing countries and the industrialized countries will cause great changes. It is impossible to anticipate what will determine these changes, but whatever it is, as Michael Edwardes, British writer on Asian affairs, warned, "the revolution will be bloody, convulsive, full of suffering and pain." [2]

"Colonialism" refers today far less to colonies than to the process of decolonization, which represents one of the most complex and threatening problems facing humanity. In a relatively short time, colonies will disappear, but decolonization will last for generations. The use of the word "colonization" in the latter context is misleading, but the developing countries employ it because it is significant in terms of their recent historical experience. That is why it serves no purpose to say, as President Kennedy did in a speech before the United Nations General Assembly in September, 1961, that colonialism is practically dead because less than 2 per cent of the world's population now live in "dependent" territories. The fact is that well over one-half the world population is striving for self-sufficiency and equality, and describes as colonialism whatever stands in the way. It would be a tragedy if a misunderstanding about the meaning of the word caused the industrialized countries to misread the message the Third World is trying to convey.

Decolonization, and whatever the Third World means by "colonialism" when referring to it, is an aspect of nationalism, implying a long and difficult process of change. For better or for worse, the colonial administration represented a working structure that offered a clear frame of reference, and hence a certain degree of security. Whether the people liked it or hated it, they knew where they stood, what their relations with the administration were, what was expected of them, and what they could expect of their rulers. Asians and Africans will not possess again a clear framework of moral, political, and social values before reaching viability. But between the point of departure and that of arrival, the Third World has before it the immense and stormy seas of transition. Decolonization is a process of destroying and rebuilding. Even before this, it is the creation of new men, freed from the type of mentality the colonial experience produced, of the emotions and feelings it pressed down into the subconscious.

But until this intimate liberation of the individual and the masses takes place, all planning for the future will be a projection of a view of history that colonialism has conditioned. Decolonization is the abandonment of one political structure and the search for another; the gradual transformation of an economy closely integrated into that of the former colonizers; agrarian reform; the changing of social conditions hampering progress; the decline of the former privileged classes; the training of new leaders in all fields of social, economic, and political activities. Decolonization is the transition to a new society, to new human relations, by means that are often violent and undemocratic. But as Harvard historian Robert Emerson has pointed out: "It is an immense added complication that while the democracies which came into being in the nineteenth and earlier twentieth centuries were concerned with the management of relatively simple political and economic systems in a still spacious world, the newly rising peoples seek full-scale social welfare states with most complicated mechanisms, plus the extra complexity of the drive for social and economic development, in a terrifying world of population explosion, superpowers, and nuclear weapons." [3]

The more people have suffered, the more they pursue the ideal of a world where everything they missed in life will be realized and whatever caused their condition will be defeated. The Third World, for example, equates colonialism with economic exploitation and economic exploitation with Western-style capitalism. As a consequence, even the most moderate leaders—among others those of the Brazzaville group who have opted for close ties with France—proclaim their ideal of a Socialist society. President Léopold Senghor of Senegal wrote: "We understand socialism as the instrument for placing knowledge and experience in the political, economic, social and cultural fields at the service of a 'pan-human' civilization, a civilization of the universal. It stands for humanism in our time. The Negro heritage and condition are no longer negative but positive. While representing still the totality of the political, moral, social and cultural values of the black world, they no longer are founded upon color but rather upon geography and history, both political and economic. The cultural values of the heart are the contributions of the new Negroes to the confluence of the giving and the receiving, to the converging forces of socialization, that is, to a socialism adapted to our time." [4]

Socialism is seen simply as everything that colonialism was not—the way to a better social order, in which social and economic inequalities will be abolished. It preaches a world brotherhood of equal nations irrespective of power, color, or stage of development. It looks forward to a tomorrow of happiness for all. A great number of new countries find in it an answer to their hope of equality. Whether some of the leaders actually believe in the doctrine they preach is beside the point. The fact is that only by proclaiming their devotion to socialism can they hope to get the ear of the masses. That is why a vast majority of Third World governments, irrespective of whether they are parliamentarian, oligarchic, authoritarian, or military, say they are founded on a "genuine" Socialist tradition. Socialism is both a program of decolonization and an aspect of anticolonialism.

Third World "socialism" expresses the feelings of poor, proletarian nations. They are "proletarian" because conscious of their poverty; because their vision of the world is conditioned by the invisible line dividing the poor countries from those that are rich. They react today much as the working classes of Europe did during the last century when they were struggling to assert their rights. The sight of rich nations spending fantastic sums on means of destruction in order to perpetuate their world-threatening quarrels, while a majority of humanity is not even properly fed, produces the same type of reaction that led individuals, resenting or suffering from the concentration of financial power and from waste by a few families or groups amid widespread poverty, to advocate radical political solutions. Poor nations like poor individuals have a different way from the wealthy of looking at problems. They are first of all concerned with physical survival and anything that distracts from this basic necessity is irrelevant and evil.

The Third World may set itself against the rich countries not only for economic, but also for political and moral reasons. The struggle against colonialism was carried out in the name of Western principles, imported and instilled by the colonizers themselves. Freedom followed a revolution that had its origins in the West. But as the Asians and Africans strive to find themselves, and evolve political structures that are likely to work under the new conditions, and that spring from a local rather than from an alien tradition and way of life, decolonization may increasingly become identified with de-Westernization. Nearly all the present Third World leaders are Western-educated, but most of their successors will not be. The new generation will not be the product of colonialism but of decolonization; it will inevitably be affected by the uncertainties and wariness that the process of transition is bringing about. The transition is conditioned by so many factors beyond the Third World's capacity to control that decolonization breeds intolerable tensions. People may find that anything is better than their present condition.

Third World attitudes toward colonialism today stem principally from the process of decolonization. The continued existence of colonies merely helps to aggravate the problem and retard the process of transition. It nourishes Third World fears that history may repeat itself, that something may happen to return a number of the weaker countries to a condition of dependence. So long as colonies exist within their continents, Asians and Africans will feel as threatened as medieval Europe did when the Moslems controlled Spain. This fear, in turn, contributes to the urge to keep alive the same revolutionary forces that brought liberation to Asia and Africa. They are considered the only guarantee that colonialism of the old kind will disappear before too long. Some of the more moderate leaders, seeing how new nations join the international community every year, will even admit that contact with the West has been beneficial in many ways, bringing material achievements that today enable the two continents to undertake the effort of catching up with the West. They do not want to see these achievements swept away by anticolonialism; that would represent a serious retrogression for the Third World.

This concern was well expressed by Minister Ahmed ben Salah of Tunisia: "Lest it lead backward, to a regression, decolonization must not be a process inverse to that of colonialism. The failure of several countries formerly under colonial status is due to this superficial, negative and sterile approach. Decolonization must first of all mean a radical transformation of mental, moral, social, and economic structures. This transformation is not the same as destroying the positive contributions of colonialism. It means rather to ultilize and reorient what is good in them, to use them as an instrument no longer connected with colonialism but capable of receiving a new direction." [5] This program is shared by a large number of statesmen and intellectuals who have felt the transforming impact of colonialism. But they represent a small, even if vocal, minority. By and large, the masses were not affected by contact with the West and for them life went on unchanged. What conditions their outlook during the formative transision years is principally whatever in their own past colonial experience offended their dignity. Far more than the transformations brought about by colonialism, the type of human relations it established is fixed in their memory.

It is mainly to these relations that the word "colonialism" applies today. Conversely, "anticolonialism" refers primarily to whatever initiative is likely to erase forever the policies, attitudes, and psychological approaches that the Third World connects with the colonial period. The implication of this attitude is that what the Third World considers colonialism will long outlive the last colony. The one experience that more than any other helps to keep alive the humiliations of the past is racialism. It has left a deep mark in all colored peoples, extremists and moderates alike. Here is what a very good friend of the West, General Carlos Romulo of the Philippines, had to say on the subject of racial equality in a speech before the Bandung conference: "This is a touchstone, I think, for most of us assembled here and the peoples we represent. The systems and the manners of it have varied, but there has not been and there is not a Western colonial regime, which has not imposed, to a greater or lesser degree, on the people it ruled, a doctrine of their own racial inferiority. We have known, and some of us still know, the searing experience of being demeaned in our own lands, of being systematically relegated to subject status not only politically and economically and militarily—but racially as well. Here was a stigma that could be applied to rich and poor alike, to prince and slave, bossman and workingman, landlord and peasant, scholar and ignoramus. To bolster his rule, to justify his own power to himself, Western white man assumed that his superiority lay in his very genes, in the color of his skin. This made the lowest drunken sot superior, in colonial society, to the highest product of culture and scholarship and industry among the subject people." So strong do the Asians and Africans feel about racism that General Romulo warned them not to fall themselves into the "racist trap." "We will do this," he stated, "if we let ourselves be drawn insensibly—or deliberately—into any kind of counterracism, if we respond to the white man's prejudice against us as non-whites with prejudice against whites simply because they are white. . . . There is no more dangerous or immoral or absurd idea than the idea of any kind of policy or grouping based on color or race as such. This would, in the deepest sense, mean giving up all hope of human freedom in our time." Warnings of this kind were given frequently in recent years, particularly during periods of anticolonialist tensions.

The problem of racialism is extremely complex and, given the present state of human relations, almost insoluble. It will take a new world outlook, a new interpretation of the process of history, such as the industrialized countries are not today prepared to undertake, before a new relationship dawns among different races.

The problem is especially acute in those territories situated mostly in the central and southern part of the African continent, where a combination of strong economic interests and a large white minority of settlers strive to preserve the control of government through discriminatory measures against the African majority. In other parts of the continent, notably in North Africa, efforts were made to facilitate the coexistence of different races. It is difficult to foresee whether the experiment will succeed in the long run. Multiracial societies lack a common allegiance and a common ideal capable of cementing them together. The white man, who went to Africa to rule and exploit, would have to accept a marginal existence within a society trying to evolve an "African personality." He could never be a Nigerian or an Angolan or a Rhodesian in the way Africans are, since this would mean adapting to standards he cannot accept. Both he and the African are passionately attached to their respective personalities and identities. Racial distinction inevitably becomes the dominant element in their relations.

Racialism is so pervasive because it encompasses man's total personality. The African or the Asian can never hope to progress, to belong to the modern world, unless he first finds himself, and within himself the means for his own salvation. He thirsts for self-respect, dignity, and a position of full equality. He claims these things even more than economic assistance because without them he is not even a human being. "People do not like being exploited," W.

R. Crocker wrote, "but they can put up with it. What they cannot put up with is being considered inferior." [6] The Africans, having been the last to join the community of independent peoples and being particularly exposed to the evils of racialism, are more eager than others to do away with the discriminatory heritages of the colonial era. Here are statements by Africans of varied background and political orientation:

"Our fight against colonialism is not based on revengefulness. It derives from the determination to put an end to humiliation, to human slavery. Its aim is the liberation of man." (President Modibo Keita, Mali.)

"When we speak of the betterment of man's life, we mean not merely the economic improvement of living standards; we refer, in addition, to the spiritual conditions in which man lives, for just as a man without means to feed his hunger and to clothe his nakedness can take no pride in his existence as a human being, so, also, is one who is reviled and discriminated against because of his race or religion robbed of his self-respect and human dignity." (Haile Selassie, Emperor of Ethiopia.)

"The burning desire of the African peoples all over the continent for human rights, for dignity and for independence has never been so manifest as in the past few years." (President Kwame Nkrumah, Ghana.)

"In the turmoil of revolution, the basis for peace and brotherhood in Africa is being restored by the resurrection of national sovereignty and independence, of equality and the dignity of man." (Albert Luthuli, Republic of South Africa, Nobel Peace Prize winner for 1960.)

"In its essence nationalism has been for all of us former

colonized peoples a fight for man's dignity in all its aspects. Colonialism on the other hand treads under foot this fundamental attribute of the human personality." (President Habib Bourguiba, Tunisia.)

These themes recur in countless statements and declarations by Third World leaders. They reflect an aspiration to change the patterns of human relations, to build for them a foundation free from racialism and other forms of inequality. Colonialism is fundamentally the denial of this aspiration, and that is why the Third World is almost obsessed by it. What the Third World calls colonialism reflects first of all the survival of an emotional resentment against peoples who deny to Asians and Africans the dignity of equals, not only man to man, but also nation to nation, by not taking into sufficient account the views and aspirations of the emerging countries and by acting as though Europe and North America were always the center of the world.

It is not easy for Westerners to understand the Africans' and Asians' way of considering their own problems and those of the world because there is no similarity of past experiences. Colonialism refers exclusively to a historical experience which is common to the developing countries, but which the industrialized countries have escaped. The latter have never known throughout their long history the form of colonialism to which the Third World has been subjected. Before independence, the states of the North American continent were referred to as "colonies," but the word did not imply the same type of relationship toward the administering power as later developed in Asia and Africa. America, like Australia and New Zealand, was a country of settlement where people went, for the most varied reasons, to set up a new home. People came over to America to "build a new nation," leaving the motherland with the idea of never returning. At that time, "colony" referred to a body of people who had migrated beyond their country's borders but had kept a political connection with the parent state. There is, thus, a fundamental difference between countries where Europeans went to settle with the idea of making them their own, and those where they went to rule over peoples of different races for the purpose of economic exploitation and political and military dominance. That is why America's early documents speak of "colonies" but not of colonialism, which refers to an experience that began at least a hundred years later. The pattern of independence was also fundamentally different. As Vera Micheles Dean, author of a number of books on world affairs, pointed out, the American Revolution "was staged by white men against white men, with both rebels and colonial rulers drawn from the same nation and sharing the same culture." [7] The American Revolution has inspired Asian and African nationalists as an example of a non-self-governing country freeing itself in the name of certain fundamental and eternal principles. But the source of inspiration for Asians and Africans was the act of rebellion and the principles enunciated to justify it, not a similarity of experience.

It has been stated that some of the countries of Asia and Africa were themselves not immune from colonialism because they had at one time or another in the past conquered and subjected neighboring peoples. But these are no more examples of colonialism than is nineteenth-century domination of Austria over parts of Italy, or of Russia and Prussia over Poland. Italy was for centuries under the rule of foreign powers, and became independent just in time to participate in the colonial assault on Africa: yet Italy was not a colony. Napoleon's conquests are not called colonialism in history books, nor are the unending succession of invasions and suppressions of other countries' independence. At that time, rulers extended their power as far as their military strength and political cunning enabled them to do so. Austrians, Prussians, and Russians never pretended that they partitioned Poland among themselves in order to civilize the country. The Spaniards never said that they had a "civilizing mission" to accomplish in Southern Italy. Conquests in Europe were justified in the name of a dynastic or national, not a racial, superiority. The only exception to the rule may be represented by the control that the Ottoman Empire exercised over the Balkan States. To the extent, however, that Constantinople administered a part of Europe, it had come to be considered, or be treated like, a European power.

Colonialism was not only a unique form of domination but, despite its tremendous impact, also a relatively short one.[8] Third World exposure to Western ideas was too brief to change substantially the rather stagnant patterns of society. The changes more often than not occurred despite the West and were not carefully planned by governments interested in preserving the status quo in order to rule more effectively. That is why the memory of the injustices suffered is so much stronger than the "gratitude" for the benefits received. This fact also helps to shape the present Third World concept of what colonialism is to-

day. If it is true that Asians and Africans were subjected to colonial domination, those who did the subject-
ing were West Europeans only. The countries of the
Third World were not colonized by Russia, the United
States, or the Latin Americas. Colonialism is not the same
as oppression pure and simple because it defines a particular experience that no other peoples have shared.

To non-Westerners colonialism meant the exploitation
of Asians and Africans by Europeans. In their view, if a
European exploits or dominates another of his race, that
cannot be called colonialism. The same applies to the exploitation or domination of Africans by Africans, or Asians
by Asians. The intervention of the Soviet army in Hun-
gary to suppress the 1956 rebellion was a terrible thing,
but to Africans and Asians it was not colonialism. Western efforts to brand certain Soviet policies as colonialism
have proved useless, even self-defeating. They succeed only
in convincing the Afro-Asians that the West refuses to
understand their past experience and their present perspective. They cause anger, but no change of heart. The
same reaction is produced when the Soviet Union accuses
the United States of being a colonial power. The Third
World considers that these are efforts by the industrialized
countries to transpose their quarrels to Asia and Africa,
thus continuing the old patterns of a time when colonies
were pawns in the game of power between European nations.

The Third World is anxious to efface patterns reminiscent of the past in order not to compromise the evolution toward effective independence. Colonialism in the
classic tradition is on the way out and it is only a question

of time before it disappears completely. The same cannot be said, however, of the indirect forms of interference threatening the long and painful transition to viability which are often referred to with a word of recent coinage —"neocolonialism." When the interference is direct, it is usually called "imperialism." Sometimes the two words are used interchangeably.

According to a number of Third World countries, neocolonialism represents the various means and methods employed by the former administering powers to preserve a large measure of control over nations to which they have granted formal independence. It is seen as an "attempt to attain the same aims of exploitation as the old colonialism, using new methods which outwardly appear to be more in line with the spirit of the age" (President Gamal Abdel Nasser, United Arab Republic) and as "an even subtler form of exploitation in many ways" (King Mehendra of Nepal). The most dangerous form of neocolonialism, because the most difficult to combat, is considered the attempt to maintain a political influence over former colonies through a large degree of economic control. Nearly all Afro-Asian countries are in various degrees dependent economically upon the West.[9]

A country under severe economic subjection is not at liberty to pursue its political life in accordance with its own wishes and interests. It may become part of what has been called a "sovereignty of clients," having a "false independence," granted with the concealed intention of making the liberated country a "client state."

Neocolonialism may take the form of open military intervention, as when the French intervened against Bizerte in 1961, or as in the case of the Anglo-French attack on the Suez Canal in 1956. It is also identified with the continued presence of military bases in independent countries, either against the will of the countries concerned or as a result of economic pressures. Efforts to keep a country within the sphere of influence of a great power are called neocolonialism as well as the struggle to control a country's human and material resources. In short, anything that limits or compromises the independence of an independent country is called "colonialism" if the methods are overtly political and "neocolonialism" if the methods are other than political. The distinction is, of course, rather rough, not only because colonialism refers also to a certain number of territories that are non-self-governing, but also in that it is often difficult to separate the various forms of pressure. Quite often Third World spokesmen simply apply the two terms to situations to which they object. The Arabs, for example, will refer to the existence of the State of Israel as a form of neocolonialism.

Anticolonialism—whether it represents a struggle against direct domination or indirect pressure or an effort to erase the inequalities and discriminations left behind by colonialism, or whether it deals with decolonization or nationalist sentiments—involves exclusively the relations between the Third World and the West. While colonialism involved only Western Europe, neocolonialism involves all of the West, including the United States. It is from the West that the Third World wants to complete its independence; it is with the West that the Third World strives to close the gap. The opportunities are great, but the dangers are immense. This mass of humanity, trying to compress into a few years an evolution it took Europe centuries to complete may soon confront the world with problems of an explosive force. Peace will not be guaranteed by general disarmament or by a satisfactory solution of the German problem so long as Asia and Africa have not completed the process of decolonization and forced the other continents to accept standards that will guarantee their equality, in spite of the disparity in economic status and wealth. Considered in all its complexity, and with its implications taken into account, the process of transition the Third World has undertaken represents, indeed, a major threat to the peace. Anticolonialism reflects the urge of countries anxious to throw down all barriers standing in the way of true independence. The same urge finds another expression in the policy of nonalignment. They are both the product of the new perspective that the Third World brings to the conduct of international relations.

VI   Nonalignment

The developing countries want to be free to decide for themselves what serves the interest of their peoples, but cannot do so if they become identified with policies which, in their view, defeat the realization of this purpose. That is why they exploit the rivalries between the powers while refusing to take sides; they exploit the cold war while refusing to become participants in it.

The postwar period has ushered in a leveling process that is bringing about a rapid redistribution of forces within and among nations. In Europe and North America, it produced the disintegration of the middle classes and the rise of the working classes; in Asia and Africa, it led to the breakdown of the old empires and the rise of the proletarian nations. The interaction of these changes, certainly among the most significant of our age, is leading to a new balance of power in the world.

In the industrialized countries immense social transformations have occurred. The rise in the standard of living brought to the masses a degree of welfare and comfort that a few years ago was reserved only for the privileged few. On the international scale, an evolution has begun that will eventually lift Asia and Africa closer to the standards of Europe and North America. Properly directed and exploited, the forces unleashed by the worldwide revolution of our time would make it possible for the new nations to accelerate their developments by compressing the experiences of many generations into a few. If channeled in directions leading to tension, and possible destruction, they will retard and even defeat this purpose.

In order merely to begin the ascent, however, the Third World will first have to complete the transition to viability. That is what lends so much drama to the process of decolonization. This process, in turn, requires that the economic relations between the developed and the developing continents be so transformed as to favor its successful conclusion. Until viability is reached, the attention of the peoples of Asia and Africa will be turned—to the extent that they are allowed to do so—almost exclusively to their economic and social conditions. Concern with what assists and what hampers development is a recurrent theme among Third World leaders. This is how former Prime Minister Sir John Kotelawala of Ceylon expressed it: "We, the nations of the new Asia and Africa, whatever the color of our skin—black, brown or yellow—have one thing in common: we are all poor and underdeveloped. Centuries of servitude and stagnation have left their mark, a dire heritage of poverty and ignorance, upon the masses of our peoples. All our ideologies and religions urge us, in the name of social justice and human compassion, to rid our countries of this evil of poverty. The times demand of us that we should do it also in the name of peace. Poverty is the greatest of social evils from which all others spring. Poverty creates envy between countries and covetousness of each other's possessions; it sets individual against individual and nation against nation. From economic plenty, on the other hand—not the plenty achieved by the exploitation of men by men or nation by nation, but the plenty attained by mutual cooperation for the common good—from such plenty springs both national and international peace."

The Third World believes that the success of development and all that it implies, also politically and socially, is predicated upon two main conditions: the establishment of a climate of peace without which the transition to viability would be seriously compromised, and a far greater measure of financial assistance than has been available so far. Asians and Africans never tire of saying over and over again that only through a disarmament program could the two conditions be satisfied. Disarmament or armament race—that is the dilemma confronting the whole of humanity, but a dilemma that only the great powers can solve. In the final analysis, the new countries will succeed or fail in their purposes only to the extent that they are able to influence the attitudes and policies of the United States and the Soviet Union. That is why, even though their immediate objective is limited to the establishment of conditions favoring viability, they cannot escape the weighty problems of peace and war. They might have preferred to let the powers do the quarreling exclusively while they concerned themselves with the task of reconstruction. But that was not possible, because however distracting foreign affairs might be, the Third World has no other way of preventing the powers from interfering in its own affairs. The developing countries are still like an unhardened mass of clay that the West and Soviets would like to shape in their own image. Asia and Africa, in resisting the effort, and trying to evolve personalities of their own, are introducing a new element in the conduct of international relations. The great powers must take this new attitude on the problems of peace and war into account just as the developing countries must consider the attitudes of the powers. But in so doing, they take different perspectives and aim at the realization of different, often contrasting and irreconcilable, aims.

The Third World, for example, gives to what serves the cause of peace a different interpretation from that generally advanced by the industrialized countries. There was a time when people in the West believed that peace could be secured only through the defeat of communism, while the Communists preached the coming of the millennium following the violent elimination of capitalism. Today it is assumed that because of the nuclear menace Western democracy and Soviet communism will have to coexist, but not necessarily peacefully. Each side entrusts the preservation of its territory and way of life to the balance of power, viewed as the only guarantee of peace, or rather of non-war. This theory implies that only the countries capable of establishing the balance are primarily responsible for keeping the peace. The Third World does not deny this premise in present international conditions. It does deny, however, that there is no alternative to the balance of power. The alternative, as the Third World sees it, is a world disarmed, working toward objectives beneficial to the whole human race.

Disarmament would not only establish a relaxed atmosphere favorable to the development of the new countries; it would also release the financial resources that could contribute decisively to accelerating the process of transition. Asians and Africans have received, and continue to receive, a considerable amount of economic and technical assistance from abroad. In this respect, too, the cold war has been instrumental in drawing the attention of the big powers to the economic needs of the new nations. This aid has contributed to the progress achieved by a number of them. Even so, productive expansion cannot keep pace with the rise of population. The result is that today more people in the world are suffering from hunger and want than ever before. While a majority of humanity does not have enough to satisfy its basic needs, and strives to find a way out of the dilemma, enormous capital is swallowed in war preparations.

According to a United Nations study on the "Economic and Social Consequences of Disarmament," prepared by a committee of experts with the United States and Soviet delegates participating, "the world is spending roughly $120 billion annually on military accounts at the present time. This corresponds to about one half of the gross capital formation throughout the world. It is at least two thirds of the entire national income of all the underdeveloped countries." [1] Concerning the effects of disarmament on economic development, the study stated: "National efforts and international cooperation in the development of the underdeveloped countries have so far not brought about the desired acceleration of economic growth. A much larger volume of resources could be allocated to investments for productive development in these countries even if only a fraction of the resources currently devoted to military purposes were used in this way. Disarmament could thus bring about a marked increase in the rate of growth of real income in the poorer parts of the world. Bilateral and multilateral programmes of aid each have their own particular advantages and disadvantages, but insofar as political circumstances have had any weight in determining the direction and form of aid, effective disarmament and the related lessening of international tensions should improve the prospects for more cooperative international action." [2] According to another United Nations document, an acceleration of growth of aggregate incomes in underdeveloped countries from perhaps 3½ per cent now to 5 per cent would mean a doubling of the personal standard of living within a period of twenty-five to thirty years and a "real improvement within the working lifetime of individual citizens." [3] Yet, to achieve this goal "would require no more than the diversion of about ten per cent of the saving resulting from a reduction in armaments expenditure by one half." [4]

Year after year, when the problem of economic assistance to the underdeveloped countries is debated before the United Nations, the major industrial powers offer their very heavy military expenditure as the reason for their inability to contribute more substantially. They add that assistance in a volume sufficient to be truly significant must await the savings resulting from an eventual disarmament agreement. At the same time, the big powers are on record as subscribing to the principle of general and complete disarmament and have supported a number of United Nations resolutions to that effect. The United Nations study has shown that, given the will, there exists no unsurmountable obstacle to disarmament.

Economic assistance, the Third World feels, is not only a partial restitution of the riches the Western countries took from their colonies—something to which the new countries believe they are fully entitled—but is also a benefit to the givers. Within some nations the indifference of the wealthy classes to the poverty of the majority has led to revolution and violent change. On a similar basis, the wealthy countries cannot feel secure amid intolerable poverty. Money spent on war preparations is considered not only an investment in mass annihilation, hence a folly, but also an injustice because it could mean the salvation of hundreds of millions of people. The poor countries resent these expenditures all the more when told by the West that such disbursements are needed to protect developing countries against the Communist menace, or when the Soviet Union finds them necessary as a protection against the "imperialist" menace. The Third World views these "menaces" as artificial excuses to mask a naked policy of power and to obfuscate the real threat to peace which lies in the disparities between the industrialized and the proletarian countries.

Disarmament would thus contribute at one and the same time to the reduction of the two major threats confronting world politics—the struggle between nuclear giants and that between the rich continents and the poor. From the perspective of the developing countries, large-scale economic assistance, such as disarmament would make possible, would represent a most important instrument for the establishment of conditions of peace. By lifting the standard of living of millions of peoples it would also open up vast new markets to the products of the industrialized countries, contributing to their prosperity far more than does direct exploitation of Asian and African resources. The same point is made by the Latin American countries.

The developing countries' need for assistance is transient. The day will come when they will have to stand on their own feet, as Europe did when the Marshall Plan achieved the purpose for which it was intended. But the necessity of establishing between the developed and the developing countries an economic relationship no longer based on the patterns of the colonial era is permanent. As the United Nations study pointed out, "the political *détente* that would accompany an international disarmament program would in itself imply that nations were willing to reconsider their economic relations with one another. The relaxation of international tensions would provide a sound basis for reduction of trade barriers and for modification of existing trade agreements and trading practices." [5]

The Third World realizes that the unwillingness of the great powers to disarm, and thus open the way to conditions without which the independence of the developing countries is frail and exposed to all dangers, is due to tensions and mistrust among them. Even though the Third World is not directly involved, these tensions affect not only its economic, but also its social and political development. When great powers compete in order to promote their own cause or to protect themselves by all means short of war, they inevitably try to attract the sympathies of as many peoples as possible to their side. The struggle becomes, as it has often been said, a struggle for the minds of men.

The countries of the Third World have not reached the stage where they can be exposed with relative immunity to outside ideological pressures. These pressures are divisive: they tend to set one part of the population against the other at a time when national unity and the greatest possible concentration on domestic problems are of the utmost importance. King Hassan II of Morocco stated: "The attainment by many underdeveloped countries of their independence unfortunately leads great nations to compete not only for their friendship, but also for their support in conflicts which could in no way be of concern to them or be their own, but to the solution of which they do attach, however, the greatest price. Whatever their antecedents may be, whatever the purity of their intentions, these great nations do not succeed in seizing, with necessary clarity, the importance we attach to the absence of any interference, however small it may be, into our internal affairs." This applies in particular to a number of countries which, being artificial creations of colonialism, lack a national history, and have not yet developed a national consciousness. They are constantly threatened by centrifugal forces which become especially menacing to unity in times of stress. In the search for a personality that, on the national level, did not exist before, propaganda introduces an alien element. Tribal allegiances, regional particularities, religious fanaticism, racial intolerance come to the fore with a disruptive impact whenever solidarity weakens. So strong is the urge to seek a national identity that often the new countries look back into their pre-colonial history for symbols and traditions that can be adapted to the twentieth century and that they can call their own. Not infrequently this search leads to what in our age is a retrogression, even compared with the colonial era. It is only natural, however, for countries to try to oppose activities alien to their traditions and what is, or what they hope will be, their way of life. Whatever is "un-Asian" or "un-African" is resisted there no less than what is "un-American" is resisted in this country.

The tensions which the Third World believes threaten its future are those having a world-wide impact and posing a universal threat. They originate in the industrialized countries because only they have the power to menace the world. There is, of course, no dearth of tensions and bellicose attitudes between some of the young countries themselves. The view is taken, however, that these quarrels and clashes, while regrettable, are serious only for the parties involved and for the region in which they develop. They become world-threatening only when and to the extent that the great powers choose to interfere. The crises in Laos and the Congo, for example, became acute because the Communist and the Western countries exploited them in an effort to gain an advantage within a cold-war framework. Left to themselves the developing countries simply do not possess the power to menace the industrialized countries. They could become menacing only if obstacles thrown in the way of transition exasperated the whole or large parts of Asia and Africa against Europe and North America. This potential continental threat is the result of a condition of inequality and has nothing to do with national or regional quarrels.

With respect to war preparations, also, the developing countries draw a distinction between those that threaten the whole world and those that do not. The industrialized countries are exclusively responsible for the former, and only they can relieve humanity from the fear of total annihilation. If two Asian or two African countries prepared for war, the threat would be purely regional unless the great powers took sides in order to strengthen their own respective positions. The industrialized countries can drag the weaker countries into conflicts against their will, as two world wars have demonstrated, but war cannot happen the other way round. Consequently, all nations, whether they like it or not, must become concerned with the relations between the two nuclear giants and their allies, since the consequences are world-wide and affect every nation. When the Third World considers war preparations, therefore, it refers primarily to situations that, being world-threatening, are perforce of concern to the whole world.

This perspective is also influenced by the developing countries' experience with war. In recent years, the cold war has remained cold in the industrialized part of the world and has become hot *only* in the developing part. Both the Soviets and the West have intervened, directly or indirectly, within the framework of cold-war aims, in Iran, Egypt, Vietnam, Korea, Laos, and other places. Troops were landed by the West in Lebanon, Jordan, and Thailand to counter real or feared Soviet threats. Bloody colonial wars have been fought in Indochina, Algeria, and Angola.

All this is considered a residue of the colonialist mentality. In modern times, the Asians and the Africans have not disturbed the peace or made war upon the countries of Europe and America. They have participated in wars only under the banners of the colonizing countries. Indians fought by the hundreds of thousands for Britain in two world wars and saw action in Asia, Africa, and Europe. North and West Africans fought for France. During World War II, the Free French Forces under General Charles de Gaulle were made up largely of African troops. Asians and Africans fought as "colonial troops" in the service and in the interest of European powers. These soldiers reflected the condition of dependence of their countries of origin.

This past experience conditions the Third World's attitude toward military relationships with foreign powers. When a weak country ties itself militarily to a powerful country, a position of equality does not in fact exist. The weak becomes inevitably dependent on the powerful. Third World leaders have often argued that only alliances between countries of like strength make military sense, because only they are in a position to assist each other effectively. A weak country has nothing to contribute but men and bases. Military alliances involving industrialized and developing countries are thus viewed as leading to the re-establishment of a form of dependence that recalls closely the condition existing under colonialism.

These views are strengthened by the unhappy experience of those developing countries that have become involved in wars. Their domestic life was largely disrupted, and they have not achieved much social or economic progress despite lavish foreign assistance. They are well behind the rate of development of other countries in the same area. Laos, Korea, and Vietnam are typical examples. Moreover, their contribution to the military effort was very limited, and only direct or indirect foreign intervention proved decisive. As a consequence, decision-making moved to the capitals of the powers: Washington, Moscow, or Peking. Countries of Asia or Africa engaging in conflicts, or upon whom conflicts are forced, become dependent or protected states, and their independence is compromised.

It is against this background that the Third World views its relations with the great powers. The tensions between the Western and the Communist countries reflect a struggle for power which does not take into account the existence of the Third World. The approaches of the former countries to international problems are not considered suited to bring about a future leveling among continents or to speed up the process of decolonization today. On the contrary, such approaches distract from the attainment of these objectives without offering any practicable alternative. They are out of tune with the direction in which the world-wide revolution is leading humanity and are therefore anachronistic in relation to all that is new and vital in our time. The ideologies and political structures that will eventually reflect the triumph of intercontinental equality have not yet taken shape. These views, and the perspective that inspires them, are the main motivation behind the policy of nonalignment shared by a majority of the Third World.

Nonalignment is not a new ideology striving to find a place among the other conflicting ideologies. It is rather a political instrument used, in a negative sense, as non-identification in the struggle for power among developed countries, and in a positive sense, as an effort to defeat or reduce the impact of all that stands in the way of the realization of peaceful coexistence. Only in a climate of active co-operation among nations can the Third World achieve its full integration into One World. Until the goal is reached, however, its policies will continue to be marked by contradictions which generate confusion in the West.

The Third World has taken advantage of the cold war to protect its independence and to speed up the process of freeing territories still under colonial rule. At the same time it considers the cold war, and the danger that it may lead to a nuclear catastrophe, as the great immediate threat facing humanity, and Asia and Africa in particular. The developing countries look forward to a future in which they will not have to exploit the quarrels among the mighty in order to survive; where the struggle for power will not contribute to the threat of universal suicide. They are often charged with not living up to their ideals, with not practicing what they preach. This may be true on a number of occasions, but the contradictions into which they are forced are seldom of their own making. They result from the inability of the developing countries to stand on their own feet; from their dependence upon external factors for survival; from the pressures which the great powers are in a position to exert; from the insistence by the great powers that their own quarrels and problems must concern the whole world.

A mere absence of war is not enough to ensure the active cooperation upon which peaceful coexistence must be founded. It does not protect the weaker nations from pressures which they associate with neocolonialist practices designed to force them along roads other than those of their own choice. The developing countries want to be free to decide for themselves what serves the interest of their peoples, but cannot do so if they become identified with policies which, in their view, defeat the realization of this purpose. That is why they exploit the rivalries between the powers while refusing to take sides; they exploit the cold war while refusing to become participants in it. Having joined the community of nations only recently, they have no traditional enemies and do not share the traditional resentments and jealousies that have marked the history of the relations between the now industrialized countries. In the conduct of foreign relations the developing countries want to preserve the freedom to decide how each issue may affect their future and to act accordingly.

In this respect their attitude does not differ greatly from that of the United States during the early period of its independence. The Founding Fathers believed that the country's interest was best served by remaining aloof from the quarrels of Europe while at the same time preventing Europe from interfering in the affairs of the New World. George Washington, in his Farewell Address, admonished: "Why, by interweaving our destiny with that of any part of Europe, entangle our peace and prosperity in the toils of European ambition, rivalship, interest, humor or caprice?" He recommended as the "great rule of conduct" that the United States should have with foreign nations "as little political connection as possible" and that it should "steer clear of permanent alliances with any portion of the foreign world." This policy was followed for over a century. It found expression in the Monroe Doctrine which aimed at enabling the young nations of the American continent to develop in freedom, without interference from outside powers.

The developing countries today are starting out under conditions incomparably more difficult than those that prevailed in the United States following independence. This country was effectively protected by two oceans, while in our age distances have been practically annulled by speed in communications. Nor was it born with nuclear annihilation hovering in its skies. The early settlers had before them an open continent and depended only on their strength and determination to conquer it. Their purpose was to build a *new* nation, not to transform an ancient land stymied by prejudice, caste system, tribal allegiances, poverty, disease, and the memory of recent humiliations. Nor can the Third World afford to follow, as the United States did, a policy of isolation with respect to the great powers: it must try through various forms of involvement to press for a global approach to world problems.

As the word implies, "nonalignment" means that a country committed to it will not identify itself with a military bloc as a matter of policy, but will decide each problem on its own merits. This is not the same as isolation or neutralism or indifference. When Tanganyika became independent in 1961, its first Prime Minister, Julius Nyerere, declared that it would be wrong to describe the country's policy as that of neutralism, "for the word neutral often carries the connotation of not caring. We do care, passionately, about the development of justice, of well-being, and of peace throughout the world. We do care about the rights of man, about the independence and self-determination of nations or groups of nations. We do care about having peace both in Africa and in other parts of the world. On these great issues we cannot be neutral. But although our policy will not be one of passive neutrality it will be independent."

Mr. Nyerere indicated that "independent policy" and "nonalignment" are one and the same thing: "We give notice now that no one will be able to count on an automatic vote from us simply because we are their friends. Nor should any country which feels unfriendly toward us assume that we shall automatically vote on the opposite side to it. We shall not automatically condemn a policy because it is said to be a Communist plot. Nor shall we necessarily oppose a policy because it is described by its opponents as an imperialist intrigue. We shall look at every issue in the light of whether we believe it supports the cause of freedom, of justice, and of peace in the world."

The developing countries could not pursue their independent policy by simply refusing to participate in the politics of the powers. Participation is made necessary by the very nature of international relations, but is influenced as far as possible by the national interest. As Foreign Minister Louis Lansana Béavogui of Guinea has put it: "According to the problems which arise, our position will be close to that of one bloc or the other, different from that of one bloc or the other, or the same as that of one bloc or the other; and, in some cases, it may be the same as that of both. If we are asked what compass guides our course, the answer is peace, justice and freedom. Our position is determined solely by the objectives we have set ourselves. Such a definition of non-alignment may indeed be inadequate and trite, but it marks the boundaries and simplifies the terms of the problem and shows clearly what the issues are." [6]

The Third World is unaligned because the industrialized countries are forcing upon it problems and perspectives which it does not share. To the extent that it strives to change the direction of international relations, nonalignment becomes a policy of action. "Nonaligned has a negative meaning," Jawaharlal Nehru stated, "but if you give it a positive connotation it means nations which object to this lining-up for war purposes—military blocs, military alliances and the like. Therefore we keep away from this and we want to throw our weight, such as it is, in favor of peace. In effect, therefore, when there is a crisis involving the possibility of war, the very fact that we are unaligned should stir us to action, should stir us to thought, should stir us to feel that now more than ever it is up to us to do whatever we can to prevent such calamity coming down upon us."

The fact that a large number of countries are unaligned does not mean that they will not take sides or that they are indifferent before the great moral and political issues of our time. Some of the firmest unaligned have reacted with extreme vigor, and at times without much concern for due process, against attempts at Communist infiltration. A majority of Third World countries have close relations with the West; a few lean toward the Communist bloc. But they all insist that their connections with the powers be on a nation-to-nation basis, without concern

for ideologies with which they might or might not be
sympathetic.

There are, of course, several varieties of nonalignment.
Most of the time they reflect the ideas, even the prejudices,
of the leader or the party in power. The latter must in
turn take into account the internal needs, political orientations, and degrees of over-all development in their respective countries. The state of the relations with the
former colonizers and the progress achieved before independence also play a role. During the Congo crisis, the
unaligned were sharply divided in their support of the
Congolese leaders struggling to gain power. Some supported, albeit with reserves, the Soviet Union in its opposition to the United Nations operation; others were on
Dag Hammarskjöld's side. When the late Secretary-General
threatened to resign unless the small countries voted him
their confidence, the support proved to be overwhelming.
Despite their differences, moreover, the unaligned were
solidly united in proclaiming their determination to keep
the cold war away from the former Belgian colony. Thus,
nonalignment cannot mean giving equal consideration to
the arguments advanced by the Western and the Communist countries: to do so would require a degree of impartiality that is impossible to achieve in politics. Those in
power have their likes and their dislikes which are often
the result of personal temperament, political background,
or ideological leanings.

During the Third World's early years, a large number
of countries were inactive in their nonalignment, neutral-
ist in the traditional sense, fence-sitters, bitterly brooding
over their condition without doing much about it. The

evolution from a negative to a positive policy in a number of cases came slowly. It paralleled the exacerbation of the cold war and the progressively closer co-operation between Asian and African nations. Some leaders came up with their own definitions, such as "positive neutrality" and "nondependence." There have been several variations of these definitions, but a careful examination of the premises upon which they are based indicates that they all spring from a similar concern and aim to ensure similar results.

This background helps to explain the opposition of a large number of developing countries to military alliances and any form of involvement in them. This does not mean that the Third World is against alignments of every sort. Some of the more prominent unaligned countries belong to the British Commonwealth; the Arabs have joined in a League of their own; African nations have formed political alliances for the pursuit of common aims. The Third World's opposition is limited to those blocs that tend to divide the globe into competing and unfriendly camps. For this reason, the unaligned countries have repeatedly refused to form a bloc of their own in contrast with the Communist and Western blocs. As Archbishop Makarios, President of Cyprus stated: "The concept of a bloc would involve limitations in objectivity, the very thing to be avoided in any constructive dealing with world problems."

The unaligned countries deny the validity of the theory that the main problem of the modern world is military and consider themselves in tune with the course of events and spokesmen for vast numbers of people in the Western and Communist nations despite the policies pursued by their governments. As a consequence, the developing countries take the view that the spread of nonalignment would contribute to peace. Believing as they do that the fundamental cause of tensions is economic disparity, it follows that the remedy cannot be the amassing of armaments but must be economic development. Armaments create a vicious circle: they absorb a good part of the resources that could contribute to economic development, thus retarding it; an inadequate development, in turn, perpetuates the fundamental cause of tensions. Nonalignment is viewed as an effort to break this vicious circle. Pursuit of this policy becomes a means of active participation in international affairs, as shown by the Third World's attitude toward the cold war and the problems and challenges it poses for humanity.

VII   Cold War

The reasons for the quarrels between the powers
are not as important as the fact that they are quarreling. The question of which side is right and
which is wrong in a given situation is not as vital
for world peace as the implications of the relations
between blocs.

The new countries' attitude toward the cold war is largely
influenced by the belief that as long as the power of the
West and that of the Communist countries is kept in
balance, each bloc will deter the other from extending its
dominating influence to Asia and Africa. Their independence is contingent on this balance. They exploit the quarrels among the powers in the pursuit of objectives of their
own, believing that in the present international circumstances they are left with no other alternative. At the same
time, they fear that they would risk losing their independence if either side "won," even assuming that victory was
achieved without a conflagration. Implicit in this approach
is the rejection of the position often taken in the West
that nonalignment is a "luxury" that the new nations can
afford only because the might of the Free World shields

them from Soviet domination. Few peoples in Asia and Africa are under any illusions as to what their fate would be if communism spread its power over the entire world. They are equally convinced that victory by the West would return the two continents to a status akin to colonialism. The practices associated with neocolonialism would destroy their independence perhaps less brutally but not less surely than communism. History has taught them that that freedom which cannot be defended is not respected.

One of the main objectives of Third World foreign policy is, therefore, to help preserve the balance between the powers and to oppose their efforts to unsettle it in order for one to gain a preponderant position over the other. The Third World is drawn into the cold war in an effort to defeat the purposes for which it is fought. These purposes, in its view, are dictated by a struggle for power in which ideologies represent an instrument, not an end. Ideologies can be conveniently forgotten when it suits the great powers; the United States and the Soviet Union did so during World War II. The method of conducting the relations between states is the same today as in the past, when no one thought of using ideologies to pursue certain objectives of foreign policy. Crises have always existed, and each successive generation was told that the ones confronting it were the "gravest" ever faced by humanity. But if in the past the struggle for power had a certain logic because it served to pursue attainable objectives in a world where only Europe and North America possessed the initiative in international affairs, today it is anachronistic because it ignores the changes in the balance of power brought about by the emergence of Asia and Africa.

The present pattern—a variation of a long-established theme—has its origin in the new equilibrium that followed World War I in the industrialized part of the world, long before Asia and Africa became independent. It reached a critical stage, and acquired the name of "cold war," with the rise of the United States and the Soviet Union as atomic and nuclear giants shortly after World War II. The Third World had been born by then, but the pattern remained unchanged. Each of the two superpowers claimed to have the answer to the problems of the new nations. Both tried to gain the Third World's support by proclaiming that they were propounding or defending principles having a universal value. The West invited the new countries to join in a struggle to ensure the triumph of the Free World; the Soviets appealed for assistance in fighting imperialism and capitalist exploitation. These solicitations went unanswered because they were dictated by perspectives of the world's problems in which the new countries did not share. They implied a division of all nations into two camps, the existence of two worlds instead of three, the inability to choose other alternatives, the necessity of adapting to the problems of others. The new countries could not have responded favorably without losing their identities and becoming poor copies of older established nations.

In approaching the problems arising from the struggle for power, the Third World draws a distinction between cold war initiatives that affect Asia and Africa directly and those that affect the international situation as a whole. The former present an immediate threat; the latter a potential and frightening one. On more than one occasion, the Western and the Communist countries have tried to gain an advantage by carrying their quarrels to the developing continents. The Korean war was a typical example of involvement of an Asian country directly in the cold war. Quite often strategic necessities and the need not to weaken the Free World have been advanced by some of the powers in an effort to preserve positions in Asia and Africa. The same considerations have led to the retention of bases and military installations, with or without the agreement of the parties concerned. Efforts by some countries to gain full control over every part of their territory were rebuffed in the name of strategic necessities. The French, in their effort to achieve the rank of atomic power, have exploded atomic devices in the Sahara despite the vigorous opposition of the African countries. On more than one occasion the Afro-Asians have undertaken at the United Nations initiatives aimed at insulating their continents from the cold war. The cold war thus becomes a reason for retarding the end of colonialism and hampering the process of decolonization. So long as it continues, the developing countries will not be able to escape the pressures dictated by power politics.

Were it for no other reason than the link between cold war and colonialism, the Third World would be compelled to take a position in the relations between the contending powers in an effort to reduce as much as possible the repercussions in Asia and Africa. But the long-range implications are not less fateful because the cold war is the main obstacle to the transition from competition to peaceful coexistence, from an excessive world concern with the problems of the industrialized countries to those affecting humanity as a whole. This is an added reason why nonalignment cannot mean indifference or lack of participation in world affairs. The refusal to become identified with one of the competing blocs is as much in the interest of the new countries as is their active involvement in the relations between the powers. Their purpose is to induce the powers to renounce the idea of victory—which would result in domination of the world by a group of industrialized countries and the ideology they propound—and to induce them to accept the principle of peaceful coexistence as understood by the Third World.

The more politically conscious leaders believe that this objective can be reached by gradual stages, and that the Third World must spare no efforts to realize it. They are also convinced that they will succeed because that is the end toward which history—barring a disastrous war—is leading humanity. They find it comforting that the growing body of public opinion in some of the committed countries is not dissimilar from theirs, even though it is motivated by different considerations.

Very broadly, the steps to be taken toward peaceful coexistence are viewed as follows:

—to refrain from taking initiatives likely to contribute to the worsening of the tense relations between Western and Communist countries;

—to reduce mutual fears and to try to establish some confidence between the powers so that they will consent to a gradual and balanced limitation of their military forces;

—to keep pressing for the above objective until complete and general disarmament is reached.

The achievement of disarmament would imply a willingness to cooperate rather than compete; it would inevitably pave the way to peaceful coexistence.

The first objective is possibly the most difficult in the present circumstances because its realization is predicated upon a political prudence and an understanding of the motivations behind the conflicts for power that the developing countries do not always possess. Fundamentally, the developing countries understand their position of non-alignment as being in itself an instrument for preventing a worsening of the relations between the powers. The new nations believe that each of the two blocs is still confident of winning the competition also because each preserves the hope of attracting the Third World to its side. But if the Third World succeeded in making it sufficiently clear that it will not, under any circumstances, join one of the two military blocs, it would also help to dispel their illusion.

The unaligned countries, however, are hampered in a number of ways from carrying their point home with sufficient conviction. A number of Afro-Asian countries have chosen to become committed to the West, thus keeping alive the hope that others may follow. The interest the great powers show in the new countries is flattering and gives them a certain sense of security. The latter are often led to exploit the quarrels between the powers, and this, too, generates confusion. Occasional support of one side in the cold war gives ground for hope in a future change of orientation.

Confusion is further generated by the way the developing countries approach specific cold-war issues and offer solutions which, being inspired by their own perspective, show at times a startling ignorance of the responsibilities and implications of power, and of the close tie between the several elements which together contribute to maintaining the balance of power. A rather painful demonstration was given at the Belgrade conference in 1961. Several statements made on the Berlin question, which at the time had entered into a most acute phase, indicated a lack of understanding that certainly did not aid the search for a solution. This is what a delegate somewhat sympathetic toward the West had to say:

"We feel that until the Germans free themselves from the influence of alliances, their problem will never be settled. The right of the German people to self-determination must be recognized. The occupation that has been in force since the end of the war must be brought to an end. The problem of Germany is not an isolated problem; being a source of tension, it is of concern to the entire world. The Germans on both sides of the demarcation line must resolve to seek a reconciliation and to adopt a policy of nonalignment."

It was because of statements such as these that Walter Lippmann, who is not without understanding of the emerging nations, stated: "When it comes to the vital question, which is how to maintain the balance of power which preserves the peace of the world, the final decision cannot be left to those [the unaligned] who do not have the ultimate responsibility for peace." [1]

The more responsible and politically conscious unaligned spokesmen know exactly with whom the "ultimate responsibility for peace" rests and base their international action on the assumption that without the agreement of the United States and the Soviet Union peace cannot be established. The main task of the unaligned countries is, therefore, to induce the two superpowers to reconcile their differences. "If I select these two powers in particular," former Prime Minister U Nu of Burma stated, "it is because the ultimate decision as to peace and war rests with them. In the present situation there can be no major war without their participation, and equally there can be no genuine peace unless both of them will it. Thus they share between them an extremely heavy burden of responsibility not only to their own people but to entire humanity, and an anxious world prays daily that they will not fail to discharge their responsibility."

This position means that the Third World cannot, nor should it wish to, lay down the terms on which the powers should negotiate. It does mean, however, that the unaligned countries have the duty and the function to tell the powers that they must negotiate. The need to establish the conditions that will lead to negotiation thus becomes an end in itself. The reasons for the quarrels between the powers are not as important as the fact that they are quarreling. The question of which side is right and which is wrong in a given situation is not as vital for world peace as the implications of the relations between blocs. Since negotiations leading to an understanding represent an immutable objective, the purpose is to undertake whatever action contributes to its realization.

None of the powers has shown an appreciation of this position because it places them all in the same boat. Nothing could be more infuriating for the West than to be considered on the same level as the Soviet Union, and vice versa. The unaligned feel, however, that if when tensions erupt they directed their sympathies toward one bloc to the detriment of the other, that would complicate the problem because the other side would not feel inclined to negotiate. They know from experience that they have to deal with proud and sensitive countries. Their ear cannot be gained unless the approach is friendly. To condemn a country is the worst way to seek to influence it.

Whenever a crisis develops, whatever the reason, the most important consideration is that it means a deterioration of the international situation. Once again, who is right and who is wrong becomes secondary. Every new crisis simply represents an added danger facing humanity and serves to underline the urgent need for peace and disarmament. The important task is to eliminate the crisis in order to reduce the threat. This purpose is served only when the two sides agree. It little matters, in the opinion of the Third World, whether an American plan or a Soviet plan is good or bad. The only test of validity is: "Will the other side accept it?" If it does not, the responsibility rests with both sides, since they are both jointly responsible for the maintenance of peace. That means that though one power may break the peace, both sides are condemned because it takes at least two to come to an understanding. In dealing with cold-war problems the unaligned realize that they represent small and weak countries, beset by all sorts of problems, not free to do as they like, and even less free to order the great powers about. The forms of pressures exerted upon the powers reflect this situation and are effective only to the extent that impartiality is shown. No power, of course, is inclined to consider a country impartial that is not on its side. As an Asian delegate complained at a conference of unaligned countries: "On the one hand, we are expected to take up violently and consistently anti-Western positions on all the problems of the day, or our conference will be said to have ended in a failure for which the 'agents of imperialism masquerading as neutralists bear full responsibility.' On the other hand, there are likely to be attacks from the West branding us as 'pseudo-neutrals entirely won over to Communist ideas.' "

While the chances of intervention in situations created by the struggle for power and the conflict of ideologies are limited, because the Third World cannot counter with a power or an ideology of its own, in the crises growing out of initiatives undertaken by one of the powers, the unaligned have a certain freedom of action in their efforts to restore the equilibrium. This was shown with particular clarity in two circumstances that threatened world peace: the U-2 incident in 1960 and the decision by the Soviet Union to break the moratorium on the suspension of atomic and nuclear tests in 1961.

On May 1, 1960, a United States aircraft was brought down deep inside the territory of the Soviet Union while on an espionage mission. The Soviet Union used the incident as a reason, or an excuse, to refuse to participate in a summit conference which was scheduled to take place in Paris a few days later. Moscow requested an urgent meeting of the United Nations Security Council "to examine the question of aggressive acts by the Air Force of the United States of America against the Soviet Union, creating a threat to universal peace." In his opening address,

Soviet Foreign Minister Andrei A. Gromyko invited the organization not to evade its responsibility, to condemn the "incursions by United States aircraft into the territory of other states" and to regard them as "aggressive acts." The incident had been considered in most countries as a bad blunder, responsible for a new serious crisis in international relations. The representative of Tunisia stressed "the measure of disappointment and bitterness which overwhelmed the peoples of the world when it became clear, on 16 May, that the Summit Conference was doomed to failure right from the outset, even before any discussion of the problems to be considered had been embarked upon." Similar sentiments were expressed by the representative of Ceylon.

The two countries which, at the time, represented the Third World in the Security Council refused to respond to the Soviet request to condemn the United States. They took the position that condemnation would have merely resulted in worsening the crisis and in compromising the chances of restoring normal relations between the two superpowers. They thereupon drafted a resolution, in opposition to the Soviet text, which merely contained a recommendation for a relaxation of tension and a solemn appeal for a resumption of talks on general disarmament in all its aspects. The Tunisian delegate made it clear that "no paragraph or phrase" in the resolution could be construed "as a reproach to any member of the Council or as capable of embarrassing any member," nor was it intended to "favor the position of either party." The Ceylonese representative in turn stated that, "whatever has happened," the issue before the Council was "the resumption of good faith, good will and negotiation, particularly among the great powers." He added: "What can we do? Can we deal in any other way with the great powers? Can we do anything here and now to bring about a resumption of discussions except to appeal to them to do so?"

The position of the two unaligned delegates drew the ire of the Soviet Foreign Minister. He accused them of disregarding "the main issue, the issue on which the attention of the entire world is at present focused—the dangerous act of provocation perpetrated by the United States against the Soviet Union." He berated them because their resolution "does not raise, indeed does not even mention, the matter of condemning the policy of provocation pursued by the Government of the United States against the Soviet Union." He charged them with not showing "even the slightest degree of objectivity and courage. . . . To judge from the statements of the representatives of some countries," he went on, "the main merit of the . . . resolution in the minds of its authors, is the fact that it does not offend anyone. But that is precisely its main defect." Gromyko branded the initiative as "ineffective and empty," designed to turn the United Nations into a "subsidiary of the Pentagon."

Even though the resolution greatly displeased the Soviet Union, which for once had a rather strong case, it served the purpose for which it was intended—to avoid further poisoning of the atmosphere by condemnation of a power clearly responsible for the worsening in the cold war. The unaligned were not interested in establishing where the responsibility for the crisis lay, but only in the fact that a new crisis had developed. The United States had reasons on this occasion to be deeply grateful to the representatives of two Third World countries.

The same approach inspired unaligned reaction to the resumption of nuclear tests by the Soviet Union, especially since this had occurred in the midst of very grave tensions between the powers over the German question. Once again the unaligned refrained from condemning one side and appealed to both to reconcile their differences. From Belgrade, where they had joined in a conference, they sent a message in identical terms to President Kennedy and Chairman Khrushchev which stated in part: "Having regard . . . to the gravity of the crisis that menaces the world, and the urgent need to avert the developments that may precipitate it, we take the liberty of urging on the Great Powers concerned that negotiations should be resumed and pursued so that the danger of war might be removed from the world and mankind adopt ways of peace." The Kennedy Administration reacted with obvious annoyance at the unwillingness of the unaligned to take a stand against the resumption of nuclear tests. There were charges of double standards, the same that Gromyko had leveled at the time of the U-2 incident. Both sides in succession accused the Third World of cowardice because it refused to take a stand when a grave "moral" issue was involved. The unaligned retorted that there would be no tensions if the great powers conducted their relations differently and ceased threatening from positions of strength. In both instances, the unaligned were interested in re-establishing the balance and not in upsetting it further.

The role of the unaligned proved more difficult during the grave crisis late in 1962, following United States determination to see the Soviet missile installations in Cuba completely removed. Washington's unilateral decision in establishing a blockade was resented as a form of pressure against a small country reminiscent of practices to which the Third World had been subjected under colonialism. Cuba's revolution had won the sympathy of most Afro-Asian countries because it had striven to bring about a radical change in social and economic structures, a process akin to that of decolonization. There also was the solidarity of small countries toward another small country and a strong feeling about its right to live under a regime that one of the great powers disliked. During the early days of the Castro regime efforts were made to win Cuba over to the unaligned camp and in 1961 the country had been invited to participate in the Belgrade Conference. While saying that it subscribed to nonalignment, Cuba had in fact violated some of its basic tenets, thus compromising Afro-Asian support. It had then chosen to side with one of the super-powers, inevitably provoking the reaction of the other, and what is more in a zone of vital strategic importance to the latter. In so doing it had upset the international equilibrium whose preservation the Third World considers indispensable to its survival. It had allowed foreign bases to be installed on its territory and contributed to the extension of the area of nuclear peril.

Much as the Afro-Asians objected to Cuban policies, their main resentment was directed at the way the Soviet Union handled its relations with the island. Moscow had agreed to Washington's request for an international inspection of the removal of missile sites without even bothering to consult and get the consent of the Castro government.

It stressed that the bases were manned by Soviet techni-
cians, thus indicating that the Cubans had no say in their
operation. Throughout the crisis it conveyed the clear impression that it was deciding things in behalf of Havana
and that any decision would be obeyed. When it took alone
the decision to dismantle the installations, it became clear
that they had been set up to serve the military purposes of
the Soviet Union and not to strengthen Cuba's defenses.

At the time the issue was brought before the UN Security
Council, the two Third World representatives (United
Arab Republic and Ghana) suggested initiatives likely to
reduce the tension and to re-establish the international
equilibrium. They also voiced their concern lest the crisis
were used to go beyond the re-establishment of the status
quo ante and for the violent suppression of the Castro
regime in the island. While the unaligned countries were
pleased at the willingness shown by Washington and Moscow to negotiate a solution of the controversy, they also
considered it dangerous that great powers took decisions
at the expense of a small country.

Third World attitudes toward issues which it regards as
settled, irrespective of their merits, are often dictated by
the assumption that its intervention cannot serve a "useful"
purpose. The tendency in such cases is to abstain, a different stand being thought useless in changing the situation
and only likely to exacerbate the cold war. This was seen
following the Soviet Union's repression of the Hungarian
revolt and when Communist China occupied Tibet. A
resolution (December 12, 1956) condemning the Soviet
Union for violating the United Nations Charter and the
liberty of the Hungarian people was supported by 15

Afro-Asian countries while 11 abstained and none voted against. Another resolution (December 20, 1961), calling for "cessation of practices which deprive the Tibetan people of their fundamental human rights and freedoms including their right to self-determination," gained 21 Afro-Asian votes while 25 countries abstained.

When an issue remains to be settled, Third World countries are more inclined to vote according to their political orientation or their assessment of the problem. In these cases the number of abstentions is quite small. For example, a Soviet resolution (October 30, 1962) to seat Communist China in the United Nations received 25 Afro-Asian votes in favor, 23 against, and 5 abstentions.

These examples tend to prove that the Third World is not neutral and that it does not vote as a bloc on cold war issues, but rather that it views international issues from the angle of its own perspective and interests which do not necessarily coincide with those of one or the other of the great powers. Even though the Third World is not a party to the cold war, it cannot escape being involved in it.

While the Third World is anxious for the great powers to neutralize each other in the hope that their disputes will not erupt into war, it does not look forward to a final settlement before and until disarmament. This attitude is dictated by the concern that the powers might reach a compromise by dividing the rest of the world into zones of influence. The implications of the partition of Korea and Vietnam into North and South—following a protracted struggle between Communist and anti-Communist forces in which neither could achieve a decisive victory—the North being under Communist and the South under Western control—were not lost upon the Afro-Asians. What if the two blocs, each realizing the impossibility of imposing its will upon the other, found it expedient to settle all their problems the same way? Is not the division of Germany another warning signal? In this respect also, the Afro-Asians consider world problems in terms of their own historical experience. The partition of Asia and Africa had been the result of agreements between the powers. The Middle East was partitioned after World War I, following an understanding between Britain and France. So long as the Third World is exposed to the pressures of the powers, and unable to provide for its own defense, it will fear a repetition of the circumstances that led it to fall under colonial domination. That is why, even though it recognizes that a compromise between the United States and the Soviet Union on specific cold war issues is indispensable to peace, it insists upon participating in whatever negotiation or conference is held to implement a particular decision.

This pattern was shown in the long and difficult debate on disarmament and the suspension of atomic and nuclear tests. The unaligned were quite willing to accept any formula agreeable to the two superpowers; but once it was found, they made clear their determination to take an active part in the negotiations for its implementation. Gradually the powers accepted the premise that on issues affecting humanity the small countries of Asia, Africa, and Latin America could not be ignored or left out. In recent years, United Nations working committees on disarmament and the cessation of tests, in which only the representatives of the great powers used to participate, have been widened to include a substantial number of Third World countries. It is also recognized that the latter might play a useful role in enforcement measures such as inspection and control.

Negotiation is, of course, indispensable to prevent a situation going from bad to worse and leading to war. But, given the present pattern of international relations, can it be truly fruitful before the Third World has reached its objectives? Many of the unaligned nations doubt it. Peace depends on the elimination of potential causes of war, that is, of the division of the world into opposing camps. The threat will persist not only so long as countries are divided into ideological blocs, but also while there are such deep inequalities between rich countries and poor countries. Not only the cold war, but also colonialism, disturbs the peace of the world. Thus peace can be had only when both have been done away with. Disarmament will not attain its true objectives—a world where nations are willing to co-operate irrespective of their ideologies—before the process of de-colonization has been accomplished. Only then will a sufficient degree of equality exist to make co-operation possible.

As long as the proletarian nations are dependent upon the industrialized powers for their very subsistence, they may be legally independent but not in fact free. In this respect also the attitude of the poor countries is dictated by their own historical experience. In the past, sovereignty did not protect China from brutal plundering on the part of the Western powers. The Latin American countries not long ago possessed all the paraphernalia of sovereignty, but were in fact at the mercy of powerful foreign economic interests, and a landing of the marines was sufficient to change a situation of which Washington did not approve. The Eastern European states today are formally sovereign, but their independence is subject to severe limitations because of overpowering ties with the Soviet Union. Dependence, whether economic or political, is a grave source of conflict. The Third World cannot separate the dangers deriving from the cold war from those attributable to colonialism. It sees a strong connection between the two because both are the outcome of the same conception of international relations.

This concept, in the Third World's view, is senseless because it leads nowhere. It slows down but cannot stop the evolution of humanity toward relations in tune with the revolutionary changes that characterize our age. The two blocs risk involving humanity in a conflict which, given the modern instruments of war, neither can win. They propose to destroy each other without reason, without a valid cause. Differences will exist as long as man; peoples will always be split by different ideologies and beliefs. Moslems and Christians, Roman Catholics and Protestants fought long and bloody wars because they thought that their religions were irreconcilable, that the triumph of one meant the destruction of the others. Yet they did gain from bitter experience the wisdom to accept coexistence. They learned it when they desisted from trying to impose a religion on people who would not accept it voluntarily.

The Third World was born at the same time as the cold war. Both are products of the social and political upheavals that World War II brought to a climax. There is, however, between them a fundamental incompatibility.

The cold war is the expression of a relationship based on power politics which the new countries cannot join because they have no power. And that is why they need peaceful coexistence in order to survive.

VIII   The Third World
and the West

The ultimate responsibility for the establishment
of a new equilibrium rests with all countries, but
the problems requiring an immediate solution are
with the West. Third World bitterness and resentment are thus balanced against the West's lasting
impact on Asia and Africa. This contradiction results in a mixture of admiration and hatred which
is at the root of so many doubts and mistrusts.

Coexistence has many facets. The economic facet in the
Third World view is not less important than the political
because it represents an equally determining factor in the
process of decolonization. To become viable, the new countries must achieve economic as well as political integration
in the world community. The present policies of the great
powers and the type of international relations which they
have established represent an obstacle to the achievement
of this aim. But while the Third World manages to protect
itself in the political field through initiatives directed at
preserving the balance between the Western and the Com-

munist countries, its freedom of action in the sphere of economic relations is very limited. The reason is to be found in an overwhelming economic dependence on the West that leaves very little room for maneuver in the search for elements of equilibrium.

Seen from this angle, the relations between the Third World and the West today acquire a special significance. It helps explain why decolonization is a process of emancipation from the West and also why neocolonialism in Third World thinking involves the West only. It throws light on the otherwise incomprehensible behavior of countries receiving large economic assistance and on the "ingratitude" they sometimes manifest. The greater the economic dependence the greater also the eagerness to look for political alternatives to offset it. The West no longer rules Asia and Africa directly, but the indirect political pressures resulting from economic dependence are considered a major obstacle to a speedy transition to viability. Third World leaders insist that economic coexistence and political coexistence represent the two sides of the same coin. The responsibility of the West is in direct proportion to its economic predominance.

In the economic sphere no less than in the political, the future of the Third World is determined by factors which were established long before Asia and Africa became independent and over which the two continents themselves have very little control. In this respect also its development is shaped by the economic aspects of the struggle for power. They are more difficult to counter than the political ties. The Communist countries do not represent as much of a balancing factor in the economic field as they do in the political. The defenses raised for protection against the political cold war are not equally effective against the economic cold war. International connections are something one reads about in the newspapers; people know that they exist but do not physically see them. They see the economic connections, however, because these permeate the life of a country. That is why in most Third World countries the Soviet Union seems so remote and the West so close. That is also why their emotional reactions to the two power blocs are so different. The present economic dependence is seen in the light of the past colonial experience. How else could one explain their strong emotional resentment, the lingering fears, the frightful gap in understanding?

So long as the present situation persists, Third World leaders believe, Asia and Africa will be hampered in their transition to viability and the West will continue to be accused of neocolonialism. This does not mean that responsible leaders want to break the economic ties with the West. On the contrary, most of them insist on strengthening them. The fundamental change they demand is in the structure of these ties. They want to trade with but not be dependent on the West.

The achievement of this goal requires the same fundamental changes as are considered indispensable in international politics—not a partisan, but a world-wide approach to all problems affecting humanity. Unless coexistence replaces the struggle for power, the Third World, which has neither economic nor political power, will be left on the side of the mainstream of history. It will be a witness but not a participant. Its problems will be considered in terms of the interests of other blocs and from an angle of ideological perspectives it does not share.

Coexistence—as the Third World would interpret it—implies emancipation not only from political and military but also from economic pressures. It means sovereignty over natural resources and the independence of every country in the conduct of its economic policy. It opposes discrimination and all measures of economic policy that harm the interests of other countries. "Economic coexistence amounts to an awareness of the momentous interdependence of the world economy—of its fundamental unity in spite of the existence of different social and economic systems within the various national economies. The economic development of underdeveloped countries is, therefore, the touchstone and practical manifestation of sincerity in the policy of coexistence. As a matter of fact, there cannot be coexistence only among the great, and even less only between economic blocs, but there must also be coexistence with the small and the economically weak." [1]

The instrument of coexistence is nonalignment, in economic as well as in political relations. In principle, economic nonalignment is opposition to whatever stands in the way of economic coexistence. It does not mean merely to be against economic blocs but to pursue a positive effort toward the establishment of conditions in which economic power will not be used as an instrument of pressure in international relations. It is based on the assumption that not only peace but also prosperity and progress are indivisible.

Third World views of the present international economic structures, and of the place that Africa and Asia occupy within them, have a great political significance.

Whether or not the professional economist considers them correct is beside the point. The important thing is that they influence deeply the economic and political perspective that so many new countries have added to the interpretation of world problems. In this respect also historical experience is all-pervading. The Third World is affronted by the suggestion that circumstances beyond man's control resulted in some countries becoming rich and others becoming poor. This would amount to saying that certain races are endowed with special talents that other races lack, or that climatic conditions have much to do with the problem. The present imbalance, the new countries say, is due to none of these or similar reasons, but solely to the economic policies pursued by the great powers. Power politics were the mainstay of colonialism and are now responsible for neocolonialism. So long as they dominate economic relations, Asia and Africa will be hampered in their efforts to develop.

This interpretation of the economic gap throws upon the West more responsibilities than it could possibly have. Some countries are poor for lack of resources and manpower. It is also a fact that people in tropical climates cannot work as hard as those in moderate climates. A number of countries—those of the Middle East, for example—would be much richer if they undertook the reforms that their present backward economic and social structures make necessary. It makes little difference today whether or not those structures are the product of past colonial experiences.

Economic blocs are believed to reflect the same mentality that led to the organization of political blocs, and to the cold war. They are considered to be an obstacle to the present trend in historical evolution which calls for global solutions. They contradict the spirit and the letter of the United Nations Charter. The organization's founders, prompted by the desire to "save succeeding generations from the scourge of war," laid down for all nations the obligations to promote economic progress and prosperity everywhere. This determination was reflected in the creation of specialized agencies to further co-operation (International Bank, International Monetary Fund, Food and Agriculture Organization, etc.); in the various regional economic commissions; in a number of committees and subcommittees of the General Assembly dealing with economic matters; in the establishment of the Economic and Social Council. The United Nations Charter recognizes that "the creation of conditions of stability and well-being which are necessary for peaceful and friendly relations among nations" result from "higher standards of living, full employment, and conditions of economic and social progress and development." These objectives coincide with those of the Third World which finds them indispensable to the achievement of its economic independence. But, as in international politics, Afro-Asian wishes count very little. The great powers, the Third World maintains, are making the laws and their interest, given the present status of their mutual relations, is not in peaceful coexistence.

The leaders of the new countries cite the example of international trade and the way it is still almost entirely influenced by the policies and interests of the industrialized part of the world even though it plays a vital role in the development of the countries of Asia and Africa. Exports furnish them almost 25 per cent of their national income as compared with a world average of 10 per cent. Their participation in world trade, however, instead of increasing parallel to their need for capital, is decreasing constantly.[2] During the past ten years, the drop in trade was accompanied by an average fall of 5 per cent in the prices of raw materials, while the prices of industrial goods increased by 24 per cent. In 1960, the purchasing power of a unit of primary commodities was 15 per cent less, in terms of manufactured goods, than it was in 1953, and about 24 per cent less than in 1950. In other words, the same amount of raw materials enables the developing countries to buy one-fourth less finished products compared with ten years ago. The seriousness of the situation is shown by the fact that imported capital goods have generally contributed 30 to 40 per cent of the funds devoted to domestic investment programs.

These trends are due to conditions which are not likely to be reversed. In recent times, the industrialized countries have gradually reduced their dependence upon imports from the developing countries. Through various forms of subsidies, many of them have been pursuing agricultural policies favoring their domestic production and have been continuously cutting down on agricultural imports. Similarly, it has been current practice to raise barriers other than tariff in order to restrict imports of textiles from low-income countries. A number of products that were once imported have been replaced by synthetics. General Agreement on Tariffs and Trade experts came to the conclusion in the middle 50's that synthetic production reduced by 40 per cent the demand for natural raw materials from under-developed countries.

The new countries do not believe that they are at the moment able to meet the challenge posed by these economic policies. The international "division of labor" introduced during the colonial period turned them into producers of foodstuffs and raw materials. Their exports, limited to one or two products per country, are in turn entirely dependent upon the decreasing demand of the industrialized countries.

"Why is there so much talk about financial aid rather than the vital kind of aid—the provision of more outlets for the products of the countries concerned?" asked Robert Lemaignen, member of the Commission of the European Economic Community. "It is doubtless important for these countries to have electric power stations and new factories, but it is much more important that they should have satisfactory markets for their products. Real aid measures, those which can directly affect the main issue—the living standards of individual agricultural producers who represent 90 per cent of the population—depend on what the consumer countries can do to guarantee them a market at satisfactory and stable prices. It must not be forgotten that in some years the backward countries may become poorer by 3,000,-000,000 to 4,000,000,000 dollars, a sum roughly equal to all the aid they receive. Eighty per cent of the loss is due to the chronic weakening of raw-material prices and the impossibility of finding markets for them. That is the main problem for us to tackle. When we say so, everybody agrees; but when we suggest solutions there is less enthusiasm." [3]

The same view was taken by United Nations economists:

"It is not . . . paradoxical to argue that, if the Western European countries want to help the developing countries, they could do so, without significant risk to their own industries in the short run, by abolishing all customs tariffs and other obstacles to imports of manufacturers from the developing countries." [4]

During the period of transition to more viable economies, the assistance of the industrialized countries to the Third World in finding new outlets for its traditional products is vitally important. The long-range planning, however, should be to reduce the dependence upon commodity exports to dwindling markets. The new countries find themselves in a sort of vicious circle: they need to export in order to raise the capital required to industrialize and they must industrialize in order to free themselves from an almost entire reliance on commodities. All other courses would do no more than aggravate the problem.

To increase traditional exports while the demand for them declines would only lead to the creation of surpluses and the further depression of prices. An increase in traditional industrial production, primarily of textiles, runs into the stumbling block of quotas and customs duties. A substantially greater inflow of international capital, while indispensable in assisting development during the present phase, is no cure-all. There are times when the new countries must pay out more dollars to repay loans, in the form of profits and dividends to foreign investors, than they receive in outright grants. Unfortunately, huge amounts of foreign money have found their way into a few private pockets. When, in an effort to avert waste, the donors insist upon a degree of control of expenditures, there are outcries of interference. Assistance is urgent only to the extent that it helps to establish the conditions that will enable the Third World to stand on its own feet.

The only way out of the present disequilibrium is for the developing countries to diversify their economy through industrialization in order to reduce gradually their reliance on commodity exports. This is an immensely difficult task because of the many obstacles rooted in geography and history. The time when the Third World will have industries capable of competing—as are those of Japan—with the West and the Communist countries is far away. The new countries feel, however, that the task would be facilitated by the kind of co-operation and economic coexistence that they do not believe the rich countries are prepared to undertake. The Communist countries, they say, are evading it through state control of foreign trade; the Western countries by means of customs barriers and other discriminatory practices. At present, Third World imports from the Communist countries are only 4 per cent of the total, while imports from the Western countries amount to 74 per cent. The West is the principal supplier of goods and capital. Its economic policies are, therefore, of greater concern than those of the Soviet Union.

Asian and African fears have been heightened considerably by the establishment of the European Common Market. Its implications on trade of primary commodities and certain categories of manufactured goods are also worrying United Nations economists. "The economic integration of Western Europe is intensifying the anxiety felt by some countries, most of which are essentially producers of raw materials, at the adverse secular trend which, for the moment, we have no reasons to expect will be reversed." [6] The granting of a special status in relation to the Common Market to a number of African countries, mostly former French colonies, has placed other countries at a competitive disadvantage. In certain respects and in certain situations, the trade policies of all the more advanced countries have been rendered more acute by the establishment of the European Economic Community. The adherence of some African countries has heightened the concern elsewhere in the Third World lest the scope of Western Europe's restrictive policies should be broadened. This may add a further element of division in a continent where the ideal of African unity already has a strong political appeal.

Apart from its idealistic pull, the aspiration to unity has valid economic reasons. The economies of the African countries are still essentially colonial. "In each economy, the core of the modern sector is primary production for export, either minerals or tropical foods and fruits. In each, the main infrastructure has been built to forward that trade. All lines of communication drain down to the ports which are—save in Western Nigeria—the only really big cities. Contact between territories is so slight that in some neighboring countries roads do not meet at frontiers and telephone conversations can be conducted only through Paris and London. Inter-African trade is minimal and the earnings from exports are spent largely on the import of manufactured goods, mainly from Europe and through foreign intermediaries, and on food which a static subsistence economy in the countryside no longer produces in sufficient quantity." [7]

Many Asians and Africans believe that Common Market policies tend to freeze rather than gradually eliminate these colonial structures, thus perpetuating Africa's dependence on the West. This concern was expressed forcefully by the African and Asian members of the Commonwealth at the time Great Britain was applying for membership in the European Community. It is intensified by the fact that the West is not only the principal consumer of Third World products, but also largely responsible for the exploitation of the resources of Asia and Africa.

The most dramatic example is furnished by the oil industry. A few international companies have rights of exploring, extracting, transporting, refining, and exporting the product from the Middle East and the Sahara. Iran's experience following the nationalization of its oil industry in 1951 has shown the extent of Western control. The boycott imposed at that time by all oil companies and the disruption of tanker shipments led the country to the brink of bankruptcy. Events in the Congo and the breakaway of Katanga province have drawn world attention to Western control of Africa's extractive industries. Sixty-five per cent of the capital invested in the iron mines of Mauritania is European. The manganese mines of Franceville in the (former French) Congo are 68 per cent owned by American and French interests. A European and American company set up to exploit Gabon's iron has a 75 per cent share. The share reached 100 per cent in all enterprises totally or partially connected with aluminum as in Cameroun and the (former French) Congo.[8]

Rhodesia's rich mines are entirely in the hands of British, French, and American interests. In the largest African country, Nigeria, the import trade is still for the most part in the hands of foreign firms. Foreign interests also "virtually monopolize the wholesale trade." [9] In Algeria, and Morocco, economic life is largely dependent on French price supports, subsidies, budgetary subventions, capital aid, and technical assistance.

Of course, the countries concerned would be far worse off without these forms of financing. The need is to increase them very considerably because without outside financial support they cannot hope to achieve economic progress. At the same time, however, Western interests have not done enough to create forms of partnership and to involve local interests, whether government-supported or private, in their enterprises. The former colonies have made far more progress economically and socially than a number of Third World countries which had managed to preserve their independence. The potentiality for development is greater in Nigeria or Guinea than in Ethiopia or Liberia. The latter countries were not exploited during the colonial period, but they also missed the fermentation of Western ideas. The more a country has been shaken in its traditional ways by contact with the West, the louder the outcries for radical political solutions, the more insistent the demand for an end of neocolonialism. [10] The new generations are far more impatient than the older ones in pressing for changes and are ready to use all instruments available to them in an effort to accelerate decolonization. The trend is evidenced in the growing number of countries, once closely linked to the West, which are now turning to nonalignment.

The problem, Third World leaders believe, is complicated by the present status of relations among the powers. A readiness to change the economic balance in a way that would enable the new countries to increase their share of production and trade meets not only the opposition of established interests but also powerful political barriers. At the root of the problem, as the Third World sees it, is the existence of blocs, the division of the world into conflicting camps, the whole concept of power politics. Once again what comes into play is a struggle in which the new countries cannot participate and which, they feel, tends to defeat their purposes. Lasting changes at the national level must be preceded by a new orientation based on the recognition that Asia and Africa have equal rights and equal responsibilities. Unless the outlook is world-wide, there cannot be equality among all continents. The same principles that apply to political coexistence are valid for economic coexistence. In this respect also the new countries do not seem to appreciate sufficiently the responsibilities that accompany power, whether that power is economic or political. Merely to urge equality is not the best way to obtain it. The material conditions must first exist, and their establishment requires hard work and time. How much time depends not only on the new nations, however, but also on the industrialized countries. The ultimate responsibility for the establishment of a new equilibrium rests with all countries, but the problems requiring an immediate solution involve the West. Third World bitterness and resentment are thus balanced against the West's lasting impact on Asia and Africa. This contradiction results in a mixture of admiration and hatred which is at the root of so many doubts and mistrusts.

Once the West has realized that nonalignment is not the same as indifference or neutrality but a positive political force, it will have made the first effort to understand and be understood by the new countries. The Kennedy administration in particular has recognized the significance of the emergence of the Third World. During his Senate years, Kennedy caused an international furor by advocating freedom for Algeria at a time when the French were still bent on preserving the territory at all costs. He spoke with obvious conviction of self-determination and independence and his stand made a deep impression throughout Asia and Africa. Support for India became one of the foundations of his foreign policy on the assumption that the main test in Asia is between the Indian democratic experiment and China's communism. He agreed to neutralize Laos after the hopelessness of preserving the country officially committed to the West had become evident. His Congo policy showed awareness of the aspirations of Africa.

A serious crisis between the unaligned and the Kennedy Administration occurred at the time of the Belgrade Conference in 1961 when the participants showed little interest in self-determination for the Germans and reacted with moderation to the Soviet nuclear tests. Some of Kennedy's more experienced advisers had warned him not to expect a different stand. The fact is that the President was shocked and he reacted by stating that United States aid would take into account the political attitudes of the unaligned counries. American annoyance was increased by what people in the administration considered the highly sanctimonious tone of a number of countries that they charged with being only too ready to tell the powers what to do and how to behave while demonstrating a considerable degree of indifference toward their own domestic problems and lack of determination in solving them. The United States Congress has often reacted with irritation at the attitude of countries which seem more ready to be helped than to help themselves. In too many assisted countries political leaders live in splendor and show only moderate interest in the welfare of their peoples. Not enough is being done to further meaningful reforms to fight corruption, to establish economic and social justice, to make best use of economic assistance. These lamentable examples have served to divert the attention from fundamental problems whose solution brooks no delay. They do not change an iota the fact that an explosive situation is building up in Asia and Africa for which the West must prepare.

Toward Europe there is still a considerable reservoir of good will in the Third World. The good work done by the British in preparing their colonies for independence is bearing fruit. A number of countries have opted for membership in the Commonwealth and maintain close economic connections with the former mother country. In the former French territories a policy of integration or close economic ties with France may render more acute the problems of decolonization, but the assistance furnished by Paris is well-intentioned and generous. Now that the old empires have been practically liquidated, the problems of Asia and Africa are being viewed in a more detached perspective.

These improvements in understanding are important because the West is slowly learning the language spoken by the Third World. The gulf between the two concepts of the present relations among nations is still very wide, however. The West's efforts are pursued within the framework of the present balance in the world with a view to attracting the new countries to its side in the ideological competition with the Soviet Union. The Third World claims that neither of the great powers is even considering granting what it needs most—coexistence instead of cold war. It expects the West in particular to take the initiative because the West's interests and commitments in Asia and Africa are so much greater than those of the Soviet Union. Relations with the West involve the very texture of the new countries' life while relations with the Soviet Union are almost exclusively political and distant. This is a fundamental difference between the roles of the West and the Soviet bloc.

Relations with the West are also influenced by the memory of recent experiences that will not be easily forgotten. Relentless wars have been fought in Algeria and the Portuguese colonies. The Republic of South Africa is a bitter reminder of white man's racism. The United States wavered on many occasions between upholding the principle of self-determination and supporting colonial countries which also happened to be allies within the North Atlantic Treaty Organization. On a number of occasions the colonial countries employed United States arms in fighting nationalist insurrections.

All this has helped to keep alive in the Third World the identification between the West and violence. Imperialism and the establishment of colonial empires were phenomena of violence; so was the economic exploitation of hundreds of millions of people. According to Quincy Wright's study of war, the European nations alone fought 74 wars in the first thirty years of this century, lasting in sum total 297 years, without including the monstrous record of genocide, rebellions, massacres, and pogroms. Arnold Toynbee wrote: "Different though the non-Western peoples of the world may be from one another in race, language, civilization, and religion, if any Western inquirer asks them their opinion of the West he will hear them all giving him the same answer: Russians, Muslims, Hindus, Chinese, Japanese, and all the rest. The West has been the arch-aggressor of modern times, and each will have their own experience of Western aggression to bring up against him. The Russians will remind him that their country has been invaded by Western armies overland in 1941, 1915, 1812, 1709, and 1610; the peoples of Africa and Asia will remind him that Western missionaries, traders, and soldiers from across the seas have been pushing into their countries from the coasts since the fifteenth century. The Asians will also remind him that, within the same period, the Westerners have occupied the lion's share of the world's last vacant lands in the Americas, Australia, New Zealand, and South and East Africa. The Africans will remind him that they were enslaved and deported across the Atlantic in order to serve the European colonizers of the Americas as living tools to minister to their Western masters' greed for wealth. The descendants of the aboriginal population of North America will remind him that their ancestors were swept aside to make room for the West European intruders and for their African slaves." [11]

As Toynbee suggested, a Westerner must try "to slip out of his native Western skin and look at the encounter between the world and the West through the eyes of the great non-Western majority of mankind." That encounter is intensely colored by an experience that was mixed, neither entirely happy nor entirely unhappy. The violence and the resentment it produced are just as real as the acceptance of some of the fundamental tenets that brought the West to the forefront of modern civilization. Which of the two contrasting experiences will prevail, once Asia and Africa are well advanced in their transition to viability, will depend to a large extent upon the type of relationship that is being established now, during the Third World's formative years.

The policies the new countries are pursuing today are not so important in the long run as the kind of society they are building and whether it will be founded upon respect for certain inalienable rights, so that, whatever the various political orientations, it will have a common language with the West. The need for understanding will be all the greater in that the Third World has not yet completed its emancipation from the West, even though it strives to do so. Asia and Africa are continents in transition; they will undergo rapid, perhaps violent, changes in the years to come. They are confronted with a population problem that may become unmanageable. Should this state of affairs get out of control, the world would be confronted with situations before which present crises would pale. The danger may become such that no one could hope to profit from it—certainly not the West nor, for that matter, the Soviet Union.

ix The Third World and the Communist Countries

> So long as the Afro-Asians have unsettled problems
> with the West and suspect its intentions, they will
> also have a vested interest in a powerful Soviet
> Union.

Third World attitudes toward the Soviet Union have
evolved from a background free of all the complex and
contradictory relations that have marked its connection
with the West. Once again geography, history, and outlooks reflecting the Third World's inner structure, contributed a new and unprecedented dimension to the
conduct of international relations. Unlike the European
countries or the United States, which are far away, the
Soviet Union is a neighbor in Asia, and geographically to
a large extent even an Asian country. It is also rich, industrialized, and powerful. Despite this proximity, the
Soviet Union was also largely unknown to the Asians and
the Africans, seeming to them, for better or worse, more
legend than reality. The fundamental reason for this is
that in the past the countries of the Third World that

were once colonies had no contact whatever with Russia. During both the Tsarist and the Soviet regimes, the administering powers endeavored to prevent Russian infiltration of Asia, the Middle East, and Africa. Afghanistan had been allowed to remain semi-independent to serve as a buffer between the Indian Empire and Russia. Japan was encouraged to check Russia in the Far East. Indirect Western control over the Dardanelles had barred the Mediterranean to Russia, providing a shield against any Russian contact with the Middle East and Africa.

No physical barrier, however, could stop the legend from reaching the Third World. The year 1905 proved a turning point. A rising Asian power, Japan, had defeated Imperial Russia at Port Arthur, thus proving that autocratic government was not invincible. This event was accompanied by another, equally momentous for Asia. A revolution had broken out in Russia which shook autocracy from within. News of it spread quickly throughout Asia and the Middle East, producing a deep impression. The October Revolution of 1917 that led to the final overthrow of the Tsarist government helped even more decisively to quicken the pulse of Asian nationalism. Its emphasis on self-determination and ethnic separateness of minorities had a lasting effect. It also added to the previously purely political orientation of the nationalist movements a social and economic program. "Progressive" writing became the vogue and acquired respectability. Communism began infiltrating countries such as Indonesia and Indo-China where disruption of the traditional society had not been accompanied by social reorganization.

Moscow's position on colonialism could not fail to

establish a point of contact with Asian and later with African nationalists. Even before the triumph of Bolshevism, Lenin had argued that colonialism was the product of capitalism, and that to contribute to the erosion of the former would accelerate the downfall of the latter. Lenin stated that Russia, while politically independent, was in fact a colony because its economy was tied to the West. Following the classical colonial pattern, the country exported its food and raw materials in exchange for finished products. Russia, like Asia, was therefore in a state of economic vassalage to Western interests.

"Our policy," Lenin wrote in 1920, "must be to bring into being a close alliance of all national and colonial liberation movements with Soviet Russia." In Lenin's view the alliance with the national movements in Asia would not only accelerate the disruption of capitalism, hence furthering the cause of revolution in the West, but also relieve the Soviet Union of Western pressures along its Eastern frontiers. The elimination of Western influence in Asia became the main objective of the Soviet Union and the Asian nationalist movements. Soviet propaganda announced to the Asian peoples that "European capitalism" was responsible for their misery. The victory of Bolshevism in the world, Lenin said in 1923, will depend upon the success of close co-operation with the Asian peoples: "We shall compensate a hundred times for what we have lost in the European countries." Shortly after taking power the Soviet Government signed treaties of friendship with Turkey, Iran, and Afghanistan which, while principally aimed at checking the influence of Britain, were inspired by Lenin's anticolonialist position.

When the Asian and African countries finally established direct relations with Moscow, after World War II, following their independence, they did not have toward the Soviet Union a backlog of hatred and misunderstanding which existed with respect to the West. Their relations were free of the cumbersome burden of bitterness and humiliation that colonialism had left behind. The Soviet Union thus found itself in an exceptionally advantageous position. Not only had it been consistently against Western colonialism, but it had recently emerged as the world's second power, rich with the prestige acquired during the war against fascism and nazism.

This position was not compromised in the eyes of the Afro-Asians by the fact that the Soviet Union rules over a large portion of Asia. One may wonder why the occupation by a European people of lands beyond the seas should be branded as colonialism, while the same brand of infamy is not applied to conquests of geographically contiguous lands. Why was British rule over India called colonialism and Russian rule over Central Asia not so defined? An Asian diplomat gave the author this explanation: "Russian expansion in Asia occurred while America was expanding to the Pacific. In this respect, the two situations are identical. If there is a difference it lies in the fact that the Russians have absorbed the Asian populations while you Americans have solved the problem by exterminating the Indian natives by the hundreds of thousands."

According to Owen Lattimore, a specialist in Asian affairs, however, the different attitudes of Asians toward the Russian and British empires reflect the different process by which these empires were built.

"The Russian Empire was built by an incorporative process," he writes in *The Situation in Asia*. "All of its holdings lay within one vast, unbroken expanse of land. . . . Peoples were incorporated as well as territories. The ordinary Russian was himself a subject, rather than a citizen. Non-Russian peoples were assimilated to the status of the Russians themselves. Ordinary people were held in subjection, but a part of the ruling class of each people was assimilated to the status of the Russian ruling class.

"The differences between the British and Russian types of empire," according to Lattimore, "became of increasing importance as modern nationalism developed." [1]

Moreover, many Asian and African leaders appear to feel that the issue of Russian expansion in Asia does not concern them. In a speech behind closed doors at the Bandung Conference, Mr. Nehru put it this way:

"I submit that it is completely wrong for us to consider those territories which for generations past—I am talking about the Central Asian territories—formed part of the Soviet Union. I cannot speak from personal experience but from my general knowledge I cannot say that these people are being subjugated. I do not know. If we can get a statement from a small dissident group, that does not mean that the majority of the people of that territory subscribe to it. Because somebody whispers into our ears that his country is under subjugation, are we going to come to a decision and issue a paper on it that it is colonial territory? Obviously, as responsible people, we cannot."

When referring to the Asian part of the Soviet Union, Third World countries are usually interested mostly in the material progress achieved there since the revolution. The comparisons usually made in the West of the situation in Soviet Asian territory as opposed to the rest of Russia, or even Europe, are meaningless to Asians who judge by the present standards in their own countries.

According to a study by the United Nations Economic Commission for Europe, Soviet Central Asia "is by now much more industrialized than neighboring Asian countries, India not excepted." [2] The living standards are only one-fifth to one-fourth below those of the Soviet Union as a whole, and this "is tantamount to saying that they are on much higher levels than those in the neighboring Asian countries, and that they have improved considerably in the three decades since the end of the civil war." [3] The study considers the progress in education "spectacular." "The Soviet average is a very high standard to set for educational facilities. Even falling somewhat behind the Soviet mean is tantamount to being vastly in advance of nearly all Asian countries and to comparing quite favorably with Western European countries. This favorable comparison is valid not only for information media, but also for numbers of pupils beyond the primary stages (including part-time students) in Central Asia and in France, Western Germany and the United Kingdom." [4] Summing up, the study says: "It may therefore be expected that the impressive achievements in these fields [health and education] will contribute much to the increase of productivity over the next one or two decades." [5] Asians today are particularly interested in achieving results in these same fields and for the same reason—to increase productivity. An experience so close to their own, in space and time, could not fail to prove of interest.

Moreover, the relations between the Soviet Union and Eastern Europe are not considered by the Third World a form of colonialism. As we have seen, the word "colonialism" refers only to a historical experience and not to a principle. It means Western domination over Asia and Africa, and nothing more. Also, Third World countries do not see how nations whose sovereignty has been recognized even by the West, and with whom the West maintains normal diplomatic relations, can be considered colonial territories. The very fact that the United Nations has given these countries a place within its framework means that they are sovereign and independent. The colonies, it is argued, are represented in the United Nations by the administering powers, while the Eastern European countries are represented directly by their own delegates.

The Soviets were quick to recognize the advantages of these Third World attitudes. The first major effort in the post-Stalin era to win over the Afro-Asians was undertaken by Nikita S. Khrushchev and the then Premier, Nicolai L. Bulganin, during a visit to India, Burma, and Afghanistan, late in 1955. The statements made at the time indicated that the Soviets had a close understanding of the new perspective introduced by the Third World into international relations. Because of this, they initiated a new approach to the former colonial countries which, in its fundamental aspects, has remained unchanged to this day. The visit proved of momentous importance for yet another reason— it was the first ever paid by Soviet leaders to non-Communist Asia.

The Soviets took the position that the purpose of their first encounter with Asia was not to sell an ideology, communism, but only to initiate friendly relations with neighboring countries. They not only omitted ideological debates, but were eager to play down or dismiss ideological differences. Bulganin declared in Bombay that "as Gandhi taught in India, so Lenin taught in Soviet Russia." Not only was Gandhi no longer referred to as a "reactionary ally of imperialism," but, in the words of an Indian journalist, Bulganin's statement meant "admitting the possibility of other gods and to deprive communism of the historical mission as the only scientifically valid doctrine." The same journalist relates that when a person was introduced as a legislator and a Communist, Khrushchev snapped, "I am not interested in your philosophy. It is enough for me that you are an Indian."

The Soviets avoided ideological debates not only because they would produce results contrary to those intended, but also because the main Soviet purpose was still, as in Lenin's time, to weaken the West and undermine the foundations and institutions the West had left behind. Any success in this direction would, of course, strengthen considerably the Soviets' competitive position vis-à-vis the West. Their task was not very difficult since they needed to do no more than exploit Western mistakes and the resentment and mistrust that colonialism had left behind. Since they had no positions to defend in Asia and Africa, but only positions to acquire, they could proclaim, without running any risks, whatever the Afro-Asians liked to hear.

A few months prior to the visit of the two Soviet leaders, the Afro-Asian countries had met at Bandung and adopted the Five Principles known as "Panch Shila." They are: respect for territorial integrity and sovereignty, nonaggression, noninterference in domestic affairs, equality and mutual benefits, peaceful coexistence and economic cooperation. During their journey the two Soviet leaders proclaimed their total adherence to the Five Principles. Khrushchev stated that they "are entirely in line with the Soviet Government's foreign policy which it has been pursuing through the years the Soviet State has been in existence. . . . This policy [was] proclaimed in October 1917 in the very first decree of the Soviet Government's."

"It is in keeping," said a joint Soviet-Afghanistan statement, "with the aims and principles of the United Nations organization."

Having tried to convince their audiences that the foundations of Asian foreign policy (Five Principles, Bandung Conference decisions, United Nations aims) and Lenin's teachings were identical, the two Soviet leaders proceeded to stress over and over again Moscow's "firm adherence" to each of the Five Principles:

—Respect for territorial integrity and sovereignty: "The Soviet Union and the Republic of India now build their relations on a stable and reliable basis, on the principles of respect for one another's territorial integrity and sovereignty, nonaggression, noninterference in one another's domestic affairs on any economic, political or ideological grounds, on the basis of mutual equality and mutual advantage, and also peaceful coexistence."

—Noninterference in domestic affairs: "As for the political system of state—that is the domestic affair of each country itself. As regards political views, that is the affair of each individual. That is why we ask others not to interfere in other people's affairs. . . . We enforce nothing, we seek no political commitments."

—Nonaggression: "Neither you nor we have any evil designs against one another."

—Equality and mutual benefits: "We seek friends in the struggle for peace irrespective of whether their states are great or small, irrespective of their political views, their race, or religious convictions. . . . We stand for the equality of all peoples, both large and small."

—Peaceful coexistence and economic cooperation: "In its foreign policy the government of the USSR invariably follows the principle of the peaceful coexistence of nations with different social systems which was put forward by the great Vladimir Ilyich Lenin. . . . Choose yourself the path of development you like most. And not only shall we not hamper you but we shall help you in your good work. . . . We are ready to share with you our economic, scientific, and technical experience."

The Soviets apparently also understood what Asians meant by "colonialism":

—it refers to white peoples: they have stressed that theirs is a multiracial state. (Khrushchev: "In national composition our country is a multinational state. Representatives of many creeds live in the Soviet Union. This does not give rise to any misunderstandings in our country."

—it refers to Europe: they have stressed that the Soviet Union, in terms of square miles, is more Asian than European. (Khrushchev: "Our country represents both Europe and Asia. . . . The most important countries [in Asia] are the People's Republic of China, India, and the Soviet Union.")

—it refers to a historical experience: they have stressed that before the revolution, Russia, too, was exploited by foreigners. (Khrushchev: "In pre-revolutionary Russia I worked for the British, French, and other capitalists who had their factories and mines in the Donets Basin, and I know what it is like to work for foreigners.")

Because they shunned ideology, the Soviets succeeded in establishing contact with Asia and Africa on a basis other than ideological. That basis, in the name of which ideological conflicts are submerged, is "peace" and all that peace, from a Third World perspective, implies: anti-colonialism, dissolution of military alliances, no strings attached to economic assistance, etc. On an ideological ground, as a Communist power, the Soviet Union would be unable to identify itself with Asia and Africa; but on a different level, in the name of "peace"—Afro-Asians need to live together despite their differences—the identification becomes possible. This was the point that Khrushchev tried to establish when he declared "The word 'peace' is just as sacred for the people of India as it is for the people of the Soviet Union. This desire for peace brings us closer together, unites us, and allows us to come out actively and jointly for the peaceful settlement of international problems."

Since the United States did not seek to eschew ideological considerations in its relations with the Third World, the Soviets made an effort to convince Asians and Africans that the West was against the Five Principles. Their line of reasoning ran as follows: Did the West believe in these Principles, as we do, we Soviets could establish with the Western world the same friendly relations we have established with you, Asians and Africans. Therefore the West cannot be a friend of yours any more than it is a friend of ours, and for the same reason—because it rejects the Five Principles. The Soviets also stated: "The same nations that oppressed you and kept you under colonial subjugation are those opposing the Soviet Union today." The corollary is that the West was despicable yesterday when it dominated Asians and is despicable today when it opposes the Soviet Union.

While avoiding ideological salesmanship, the Soviets stressed repeatedly their conviction that only communism could have enabled their country to acquire world prominence. They repeatedly compared the Soviet Union's present strength and prestige with conditions before the Bolshevik Revolution forty years before, when the country was as underdeveloped as most of the Asian continent is today. This propaganda line appealed to a large number of Asians who considered Russia's former experience as being quite close to their own. It had perhaps a greater appeal than America's anticolonialist tradition, because the United States had been able to create a new society in an open, vast, and secure land, building a new world where none had existed before. There was little parallel between this experience and that of the Asian countries which, like old Russia, needed to transform an ancient society weighed down by poverty, tyrannical conditions, social injustices, and widespread ignorance.

Despite these favorable circumstances, Soviet efforts to capture the minds of the Asian and African peoples by championing the principle of coexistence have made little headway because there is a fundamental difference between the Moscow and the Third World versions. The Soviets propose a "competitive" rather than a "peaceful" version, and the competition is limited to communism and Western democracy. The implication is that the two sides to the cold war will strive by all means short of war to win the competition; the ultimate objective is to have the rest of the world decide which of the two contending ideologies it prefers. The competition is to be fought between industrialized countries with the new nations as the prize. The Soviet view of international relations does not include the policies advocated by the Third World any more than the Western one does. Its concept of peaceful coexistence is incompatible with that of the Third World's, which is founded upon the denial of ideological competition and the principle that each country can select the ideology and form of government it considers suitable, without having to choose between two ready-made alternatives, which are offered from the outside, and which are the product of an entirely different historical evolution.

Mr. Khrushchev defines peaceful coexistence as follows:

"The policy of peaceful coexistence promotes the growth of the forces of progress, of the forces fighting for socialism. It facilitates the activities of the Communist parties and other progressive organizations of the working class in the capitalist countries, makes it easier for the peoples to combat aggressive war blocs and foreign military bases and contributes to the success of the national liberation movement." [6]

The Third World's attitude toward the Soviet Union cannot be understood if it is considered from the standpoint of the cold war. It is dictated rather by an important consideration of which the West seldom appears to be aware: so long as the Afro-Asians have unsettled problems with the West and suspect its intentions, they will also have a vested interest in a powerful Soviet Union. That is why the unaligned nations reject Western efforts to identify Moscow primarily, or even solely, as the center of an "international Communist conspiracy." They tend to dissociate the two elements—power and ideology—which the West insists upon associating. Jawaharlal Nehru, for example, never treated Indian Communists softly and lost no occasion to show them his contempt. Yet, his interest in the Soviet Union as a power is as old as his interest in Indian nationalism, a parallel that clearly emerges in his books. The Soviets, for their part, miss no opportunity to stress that their country is not only the proponent of an ideology but also a very mighty power. The launching of Sputniks and man-carrying satellites orbiting the earth, the testing of nuclear devices, the threats of annihilation often made against Western countries, are meant also to "warn" the Asians and Africans that the Soviet Union represents the "winning" side in the cold war.

The developing countries will accept or reject Soviet support on the basis of whether it suits their needs and not on a particular position in the cold war. An example is their reaction to Soviet efforts to champion the anticolonialist cause within and outside the United Nations. The declaration on granting independence to colonial countries and peoples submitted by Khrushchev to the 15th Session of the United Nations General Assembly, in September, 1960, received, as was to be expected, the full endorsement of the Afro-Asian delegations. When it came to implementing the resolution, however, the Afro-Asians made it clear that Soviet initiatives were not appreciated. The African representatives, in particular, reacted with evident annoyance to the Soviet Union's bid as self-appointed spokesman for anticolonialism during the numerous debates on the Congo. They knew that the Soviets were acting to strengthen their own position in the cold war, and in the circumstances the sincerity or otherwise of their opposition to colonialism was not an important consideration. They have consistently taken the stand that no United Nations decision has a chance of being put into effect without the concurrence of the United States and the Soviet Union. Obviously, an anticolonialist initiative undertaken by the Soviets is not likely to gain Western support, and to that extent it would merely contribute to the defeat of the purposes that the Third World is trying to pursue.

If the Third World is interested in the Soviet Union as a world power, it also fears it on the same basis. The mutual neutralization of the great powers is a fundamental tenet of its foreign policy. It involves principally the two generally accepted sides in the cold war, but Communist China is also being gradually included.

The victory of communism in China was seen by a majority of the nations of Asia as a symbol of the liberation of 600,000,000 people. This view was shared by some countries associated with the West in military alliances. In 1955, the Peking government was invited to represent China at the Bandung Conference where it subscribed to the Five Principles of coexistence. The end of the Korean war had enhanced the country's prestige enormously throughout the continent. An Asian country had stood up to the West, and the West had been forced to come to terms with it after a long series of negotiations. China had proved, as Japan had done in 1905, that a country can be modern despite the superiority of the West, that it did not need to reach equality in all respects in order to be treated as an equal. That was the status that the other Asian nations hoped to attain. The example was more important than the fact that China was also a Communist state. Peking had cultivated these feelings assiduously, but in 1958 it began acting as an imperialist power, causing alarm in Asia. It gradually antagonized the Indo-Chinese countries, Indonesia, and India. China has a common border with most countries in Asia, and in nearly all there is the problem of Chinese minorities. Communist China today, is no longer considered a "big brother" by its neighbors. Instead, it is feared because of its power and its bullying way of making its weight felt. In an effort to neutralize its power the countries of Asia had at first turned not to the West but to the Soviet Union. India in particular seemed to feel that Moscow was better able to check Peking than was Washington. It was thought that the Soviet Union and China being neighbors were in a better position to keep each other in balance. These hopes were rudely shattered when Communist China began attacking India in force toward the end of 1962. The Indian Government sought and received military assistance from the United States and Great Britain. Even so, India explained the conflict as arising from a border dispute between two countries and having to do neither with ideological causes nor the cold war. A number of unaligned countries took the same view, and considering that the merits of the issue were not clear, preferred not to take sides and to urge a negotiated settlement. China for its part was primarily motivated by the determination to assert its primacy in Asia and to reduce correspondingly the influence of the Soviet Union among the unaligned countries. Frequently Peking competed with Moscow for influence among the countries of Africa and even of Latin America, Cuba in particular. It recognized the Algerian nationalist government long before the Soviets were willing to do so and always tried to exceed Moscow in revolutionary zeal.

Despite Communist China's increasingly aggressive attitudes, a large number of Afro-Asians kept on urging its admission to the United Nations. They felt that a world power must belong to an organization where it assumes certain responsibilities and can be called to account for any breach of the peace. Having become a power, Communist China shares with the other powers the responsibility for peace or war. Consequently, no major problem can be settled without its participation. The Asians are far from unhappy to know that Communist China has problems with both the United States and the Soviet Union. These problems help to preserve the balance. Should any two of these powers establish a close cooperation, the scale would be tipped dangerously in the favor of those two, provoking serious international threats and exposing the Third World to unbearable pressures. The new countries, therefore, do not want to see the problems disappear, but are anxious that they be circumscribed through negotiations. The neutralization of the powers is not an end in itself, but rather a protection whose necessity will gradually disappear as the goal of complete and total disarmament is reached. But disarmament negotiations that did not include Communist China would be meaningless. "Who can deny," the representative of Cambodia stated in the United Nations General Assembly (December 1, 1961), "that any disarmament agreement—assuming that such an agreement can be arrived at—would be considerably weakened, if not rendered ineffective, if the People's Republic of China, with all its enormous military potential, were not a party to that agreement? Who would feel secure—particularly the neighboring countries of Asia— if the People's Republic of China were free to act as it wished while the other world powers were bound by an agreement on general and complete disarmament?"

The urgency of including Communist China in an arms control agreement is all the more important since Peking is more aggressive in its ideological attitudes than Moscow. The Soviets are quite willing to let the "inevitable" coming of communism to every country in the world take its natural course, but the present rulers of China want to hasten it. They believe, not in competitive coexistence— either Third World or Soviet versions—but in the inevitability of war. This contrast is reflected in the two countries' approaches to Africa and Asia. Moscow believes that the Chinese Communists' views on the role of the Communist parties in developing countries are a threat to the final victory of socialism because the Chinese military would stimulate the "imperialist" powers to act.

"The struggle for the future social order of the state can come only after the achievement of independence," stated the influential Czech Communist daily, *Rude Pravo*.[3] "The working class led by the Communist Party must aim at

helping the national bourgeoisies to employ all their resources to the point of exhaustion in the fight against
imperialism and for the achievement of real independence." The Communist parties that follow the Soviet line
oppose the Chinese Communist view that an anti-imperial-
ist policy must be followed without compromise—by "fighting the national bourgeoisie." The paper attacked this line
as opposed to the policy of peaceful coexistence.

The polemic between the two Communist countries
serves at least to let the peoples of Asia and Africa know
what to expect. What the future holds will, of course, depend on how violent the process of decolonization proves.
Both Communist China and the Soviet Union offer the
example of countries once underdeveloped and strongly
subjected to foreign controls, which have managed to become powerful in a short time.

x United Nations

> The very fact that the United Nations is today more
> representative than it was has contributed to the
> lessening of its political effectiveness because, until
> a new economic equilibrium in the world is reached
> and the emerging social forces have consolidated
> their positions, a type of international relations
> reflecting these changes cannot take shape.

Not long ago, the initiative of foreign relations was limited
to a handful of European countries. Most of Asia and
Africa lived under colonial status; Latin America was a
forgotten continent; the United States had chosen a policy
of isolation. Today there are over one hundred independent countries in the world, all actively engaged in international affairs. The harmonization of so many new
interests and policies requires an organization where they
can find full expression. In this respect the United Nations
has proved indispensable. It has established a balance
which includes not only the great powers, but almost every
nation, every continent, every alignment.

The United Nations is to the Third World the ideal of
a relationship that could enable the new countries to find

a place in the concert of nations and to participate on a basis of equality in the conduct of international affairs, with due regard to the needs and aspirations of a majority of humanity. It could also represent an important instrument for the attainment of the fundamental aims of the new nations. There is nothing in its Charter's rules of conduct that is not perfectly adaptable to an international society founded upon peaceful coexistence. All states are recognized as having the same rights and obligations and sovereign equality, irrespective of size or strength. "Faith in fundamental human rights, in the dignity and worth of the human person, in the equal rights of men and women and of nations large and small" is reaffirmed together with the promotion of social progress and better standards of life in larger freedom. Members agree "to practice tolerance and live together at peace with one another as good neighbors." The same conformity with the principles of coexistence is found in the purposes of the United Nations as defined in the Charter: to maintain international peace and security; to develop friendly relations among nations based on respect for the principle of equal rights and self-determination of peoples; to achieve international cooperation in solving international problems of an economic, social, cultural, or humanitarian character; to be a center for harmonizing the actions of nations in the attainment of these common aims.

All countries have a right to belong to the organization irrespective of the form of government or the ideology they have adopted. The principle of universality was long contested, but it prevailed in the end. The Third World strongly supported it in the long debates for the admission of Communist China. "The ideological principle as a basis for representation or admission," stated the delegate of Ghana in the General Assembly (December 4, 1961), "could be applied by any one of the big powers to block the admission of a new African state or other states in the future if, at the time of independence, the state concerned happened to have a political or social system which was not liked by one of the big powers."

By subscribing to these principles every nation implicitly accepts coexistence as an ultimate objective. In this the Third World finds reasons for confidence that the type of relations without whose eventual adoption its very existence would be menaced will one day be not only preached but also practiced. As U Nu said, "peaceful coexistence and a successful United Nations go hand in hand."

Between the ideal and the reality, however, the gap is still wide. The balance established within the United Nations does not reflect the actual relations between the industrial countries and the proletarian nations. The Third World is anxious to bring the reality closer to the ideal. Imperfect as it is, the organization has already played an essential role in enabling the new countries to assume their share of responsibility in world affairs. In fact, it is doubtful whether, under different circumstances and given their present stage of development, they could have had a meaningful foreign policy. Had the organization not existed, small, far away countries like Ceylon or the Ivory Coast could not have participated fully in international affairs. Their contacts with other countries would have been strictly limited to matters of mutual interest, and their range of participation in policy-making would not have extended much beyond the region where they are located. None of the great powers would have cared much about how the new countries felt about problems such as those stemming from the cold war or matters having a world-wide significance, such as disarmament. In times past, no one was interested in knowing what Liberia, one of the few independent countries in Africa, had to say concerning problems that the powers considered their exclusive responsibility; nor would Liberia ever have dreamed of expressing an opinion.

Today, the small countries can take a stand on the great issues of our age and be heard because—and only because—these issues are brought to the United Nations for debate and consideration. For the first time in history, all countries have an equal chance to speak up and to vote on the most varied issues affecting every aspect of human relations. This is true of all small countries, even those outside the Third World. What, for example, would be the limits of Ireland's foreign policy if the organization did not exist? Probably its relations with neighboring Great Britain and its claims over the northern part of the island. On these issues it would have been recognized as having a right to a policy, but on others of wider import its influence would have been nil. Yet, because of its membership in the United Nations, Ireland was able to propose some very significant initiatives in the field of disarmament, to participate with troops and experts in the Congo operation, to express an opinion on matters ranging from the admission of Communist China to the status of women.

The new nations, of course, are not allowed to forget that there is a big difference between adopting and implementing decisions. They know that a decision does not stand a chance of being enforced without the concurrence of the United States and the Soviet Union. They also know that if either of the two superpowers left the organization, it would crumble. Through daily contact with the powers, they have learned these and other lessons of international life. They have become aware of the responsibilities of power and of the awful burden it places on the nations that wield it. The United Nations has proved to be an irreplaceable school where the new nations have had an opportunity to become acquainted with the ways of the older ones. It has enabled them to acquire a world outlook, to understand how complicated the world is, and how arduous is the search for a solution to its many ills. It has also served as a training ground for a whole crop of new diplomats hastily recruited from varied and incredible backgrounds and sent to new posts where they brought a far wider experience than would have been otherwise possible to acquire so quickly. This schooling has been particularly important to the new African countries which, because of their previous isolation, were inclined to view only the problems of their own continent as worthy of the world's attention. They were brash, aggressive, impatient of details, as the Asian countries were when they joined the organization; but time and experience have mellowed them. The way they vote is far more carefully considered than the speeches they deliver, which are intended mostly for home consumption.

At the United Nations, the Asians and the Africans met for the first time on a basis of equality not only the representatives of other continents—they also met each other.

There they found the means of expressing their solidarity
and sought ways of acting in concert. Significantly, the
Afro-Asian group came into existence in December, 1950,
with a view to agreeing on a policy on the Korean war.
A cold war, and not a colonial issue, was therefore responsible for its formation. Early in its history, the group was
composed only of Asian and Mideastern countries; Africa
had not yet acquired a political identity. When the United
Nations was founded, Africa was represented by Egypt,
whose outlook was purely Mideastern; Liberia, which was
considered an American dependency; the isolated kingdom
of Ethiopia; and the Union of South Africa, a country
ruled entirely by a European minority. So much were
Liberia and Ethiopia outside the new currents of African
nationalism that, when the group was formed, they gave
no thought to participating. They adhered only five years
later, after the Bandung Conference had spotlighted Africa
and its problems. Libya, Tunisia, and Morocco joined in
1956; Ghana and Sudan in 1957; Guinea in 1958. This slow
growth was followed in 1960 by an avalanche which more
than doubled African representation. At the end of 1962,
the group was composed of 32 African and 22 Asian countries,[1] that is, half the total United Nations Membership.
The Africans have formed a group of their own within the
Afro-Asian group in order to coordinate their policies
toward their continent.

To say that the United Nations made it possible for the
new countries to have a foreign policy means that it also
enabled a large number of them to be unaligned. As Habib
Bourguiba stated: "If the United Nations were to disappear, our only protection and defense would be to form

a bloc of the weak, which would not necessarily save us from the strong, or else to join one or the other of the two great blocs, which would inevitably result in our being dragged into war." Nonalignment finds an expression in the voting record on countless issues. Within the organization it becomes an active policy and not merely a refusal to join this or that military bloc. Some countries will express it by siding with one bloc while others will go along with the opposite side, but none of them will vote consistently with one bloc as a matter of national policy. In judging each problem on its own merits, the unaligned country is, of course, influenced by its own political preferences and ideological orientations. But neither of the two blocs can take an unaligned vote for granted, and this is the main difference between an unaligned and a committed country. An analysis of 80 of the most important roll-call votes in the 15th and 16th General Assemblies made by Francis O. Wilcox, former Assistant Secretary of State for International Organization Affairs,[2] shows that the percentage coincidence of the 11 Arab states with the United States was lowest (U.S., 11.6 per cent; USSR, 40.5 per cent); the 23 African countries voted the same way as the United States 30.7 per cent of the time and supported the Soviet position 24.4 per cent of the time; the figures for the 9 Asian states were 19 per cent for the United States position and 34.2 per cent for the Soviet position. Most significant is the fact that the votes of the unaligned differed from both the Soviet Union and the United States nearly one-third of the time. "As these figures stand," Wilcox commented, "they obviously give an oversimplified picture of the voting position of the nonaligned countries. In a good many instances when their votes happened to coincide with the Soviet Union's, it is misleading to say that they have supported the USSR. It would be more correct to say that the Soviet Union, usually quick to seize an opportunity to curry favor with the nonaligned states, has frequently identified itself with their position in order to further its own political purposes." [3]

The United Nations also played a major role in the transition from colonial status to independence. It furnished a forum which enabled the non-self-governing countries to make their claims known and to seek and receive support. Except for Algeria, the African nations now members of the organization did not have to engage in bloody rebellion to attract world attention to their aspiration to independence. They found spokesmen in a number of countries that had just emerged from a condition akin to theirs and were anxious to dedicate all their energies to the cause of anticolonialism. The United Nations was born at the time when the impact of the world-wide revolution brought to a climax by World War II was deeply felt in every continent. The old empires were nearly intact when the Charter was signed, but there was no mistaking the wind of change blowing over Asia and Africa. It was clear even then that the age of empires had come to an end. Unlike the League of Nations which was generally unconcerned with the colonial problem and had given no sanction to the principle of self-determination, the United Nations became involved in it from the very beginning. For the first time, the colonial issue was internationalized and recognized as the responsibility of the whole world and not only of the colony-possessing countries. In 1941, the

Atlantic Charter expressed international concern for the well-being of "all men in all lands." At Yalta (February, 1945) it was agreed that the United Nations Conference on International Organization to be convened in San Francisco on April 25, 1945, should undertake discussions of the principles and machinery of Trusteeship. At the conference itself, the development of general principles was extended to apply to other dependent territories as well. Chapter XI of the Charter, entitled "Declaration Regarding Non-Self-Governing Territories," "marks the first international declaration of principles for all dependent territories of the world." [4]

It recognizes the principle that the interests of the inhabitants of non-self-governing territories are "paramount," and as a "sacred trust" the obligation to promote to the utmost the well-being of the inhabitants of these territories. It places upon the administering countries the obligation to "develop self-government, to take due account of the political aspirations of the people, and to assist them in the progressive development of their free political institutions, according to the particular circumstances of each territory and its peoples and their varying stages of advancement."

The wind of change was felt at the time the Charter was signed, even though no one could forecast at what speed it would blow within a few years. The support that the few Asian countries which first entered the organization were able to give to peoples still under colonial domination might have proved insufficient had it not been for the cold war. The Soviet Union and the Eastern European countries backed the cause of independence for the colonies not only in the hope of weakening the West's position in Asia and Africa, but also in order to reduce the proportion, and therefore the role, of the Western and Latin-American countries within the organization. Communist support contributed to some extent to the Western decision to act so as to avoid pushing the countries seeking independence to the "other side." The Africans meant, however, to exploit the struggle for power, not to be exploited by it. Upon achieving independence the problem became how to keep from their continent the cold war that had proved to be so useful up to that moment. The task might have been impossible had it not been once more for the United Nations. It may be added that the future of the United Nations depended upon accomplishment of the task.

The great powers can do without the organization in conducting their foreign relations; the small countries cannot. The latter found within the United Nations the strength they would otherwise entirely lack. Because the world body means so much to them, they also have, or should have, a greater interest in keeping it alive and strengthening it. The late Secretary-General Dag Hammarskjöld tried to shape his policy for the United Nations on this assumption. The organization was to be an independent force in the world arena, ever ready to reduce the areas of tension. He knew that the realization of this plan was dependent upon support from the small nations, and that their support was in turn dependent upon the organization's success in keeping the cold war away from Asia and Africa. Against this wide perspective, the relationship between Africa and the United Nations became of primary importance. The developing of the one was to contribute to the strengthening of the other. Mr. Hammarskjöld expressed the "firm conviction" that the African states could not render themselves and their peoples a greater service than to foster their solidarity, while "the organization must further and support policies aiming at independence, not only in the constitutional sense but in every sense of the word, protecting the possibilities of the African peoples to choose their own way without undue influence being exercised and without attempts to abuse the situation." [5] African solidarity was to lend the Secretary-General the moral authority he needed to keep the great powers from interfering in the affairs of the continent.

Things did not turn out the way the late Secretary-General had hoped. The United Nations intervention in the Congo occurred shortly after the collapse of the Paris Summit Conference in May, 1960, with the ensuing resumption of bitter recrimination between the Soviet Union and the United States. The return to acute tension between the two powers undermined the very basis upon which Mr. Hammarskjöld's African policy was founded. In the circumstances, only the solidarity of all African countries might have served to surmount the crisis, but the Africans were torn between different and contrasting interpretations of what the United Nations' role in Africa should have been. The great powers exploited these differences to pursue aims of their own and Mr. Hammarskjöld's efforts to make them desist resulted in a concerted Soviet move to unseat him. Mr. Hammarskjöld believed that neutrality for the new nations was not only in their own interest, but also in the interest of the great powers and, ultimately,

of the United Nations. He did not, however, take into sufficient account the fact that nonalignment is not neutrality. It does not mean remaining outside the quarrels of the
great powers nor that, so long as the West preserves such
a strong position in their continent, the Africans will not
seek the balancing support of the Soviet Union.

The Congo operation and the admission of a crop of
new African states occurred during the same year. The
two events caused a deep reorientation in the organization
which is today what it was probably meant to be—not an
independent force in the world arena, but the sum total
of all member states. The United Nations was no longer
what it had been up to that time. The Afro-Asians and
the great powers deepened their mutual incompatibility
concerning the approach to international problems. Given
their numerical strength, the Afro-Asians were in a position to block the adoption of any resolution or decision
which they considered contrary to their interest. The powers, in turn, could circumvent this obstacle by acting outside the framework of the organization whenever they
considered it convenient. The progressive disillusionment
with the capacity of the United Nations to act in the political arena invited the tendency to adopt abstract proc-
lamations more adapted to evasion of concrete issues than
to the facing of them, and to the setting of noble but distant goals that every country is free to interpret in the
light of its own national interests. The very fact that the
organization is today more representative than it was has
contributed to the lessening of its political effectiveness
because, until a new economic equilibrium in the world is
reached and the emerging social forces have consolidated

their positions, a type of international relations reflecting these changes cannot take shape. A trend in this direction is becoming identifiable in divisions along economic lines. As a consequence, the United Nations more and more resembles the traditional European parliaments where political parties reflect economic interests and outlooks.

The process will become even more marked with the progress of the European Economic Community, the efforts by the United States to reach a working economic relationship with its European allies, the progressive integration of the Soviet economy into the wold economy, the stages of decolonization in the developing countries. Economic interests often bring the countries of Asia and Western Europe together on political issues. Europe's increasing liberalism and Asia's increasing maturity also assist this contact. The Latin Americans follow a line not dissimilar from the Afro-Asians in most problems affecting economic development and the equalization between the poor and the industrialized countries. On political issues they support anticolonialism except for those countries which, fearing that Asia and Africa may eventually replace them as suppliers of raw materials and basic commodities, prefer to side with Europe. The various Economic Commissions established by the United Nations in nearly all continents are proving far more effective and efficient than their political counterparts.

The new nations have contributed considerably to this realignment within the United Nations. Undergoing as they do a process of decolonization which consists primarily in achieving an economic revolution that will give substance to their political independence, their concern is directed to their relations with the industrialized countries and the political obstacles that stand in the way. While a solution of the cold war would relieve humanity of a frightening but useless threat, integration of the continents after a closing of the gap between them would result in a new direction and a synthesis that would open a new chapter in human evolution. The cold war is for the great powers to settle, but the process of integration requires the joint effort of all countries in the world. The Third World can exploit the former, or assist in its solution, but it can *participate* only in the latter.

The United Nations' framework makes this participation possible; it offers the rich and the poor countries an opportunity to meet and to undertake together an effort of understanding. Despite their contrasting ideologies, the methods employed by the Western and the Communist countries in conducting international affairs are remarkably similar. They are based on the assumption that only the countries possessing the most power can have a final say. Neither of the two blocs, however, knows much about what the Third World wants and what it expects of them. Normal diplomatic contacts, being mostly confined to problems arising between two countries or to matters concerning their mutual interests, are not sufficient to improve the acquaintance. At the United Nations, on the other hand, all new countries make their position known at the same time on all issues that come up for debate. This procedure reveals not only the feelings of one or the other country about a given issue, but the fundamental approach to the main issues of our age. In other words, the industrial and the new poor countries learn how their respective minds function. Between the two large groupings, the problem is not so much one of surmounting their mutual incompatibilities as of removing their mutual misunderstandings. Today, the industrialized countries find the new nations less mysterious, less incomprehensible, than was the case only a few years ago. There is a better knowledge and appreciation of what makes the Third World tick.

In their policy-making the powers have shown that they realize they cannot afford to ignore a group of countries representing a majority of the world's population. They must, if not consult, at least explain; try to win the developing countries over to their way of thinking; disprove the position of their antagonists. To this extent, the rich countries need the United Nations as much as the poor ones do. But there is another compelling reason. Because the small countries must have the United Nations in order to be heard and in order to elaborate a foreign policy, no power can weaken the organization or compromise its existence without incurring their ire. Even those countries which have preserved or established a close connection with a Western power through bilateral agreements are anxious to know that they can have recourse to the organization if they feel that the agreements have been violated or if the spirit in which they were entered into changes. It is quite possible that those same countries might have been very reluctant to establish an intimate contact with a power if they lacked the security of membership in the United Nations.

There are, of course, different and contrasting interpretations about what helps to strengthen and what to weaken the world body. The new countries are often lectured by the powers on the way to behave or not to behave if they really want to increase the prestige of the organization. Even when the criticism is sincere, it reveals a different interpretation of the aims of, and hence the approach to, international action. It is significant that even though the powers could do without the organization, none of them has so far left it. Under the presidency of Charles de Gaulle, France scorned the United Nations; the Republic of South Africa has been attacked at every session because of its policy of apartheid; Portugal, under Antonio Salazar, threatened to walk out because of the hostile attitude adopted by a majority of the General Assembly toward its colonial policies. Despite what some countries have felt to be extreme provocations, they have realized the dangers of remaining isolated in a critical age of transition such as ours.

Were it for no other reason than that it has offered a framework wherein a new synthesis can be elaborated, and a point of contact established between different mentalities and approaches, the United Nations would still have accomplished a historic mission. In the long perspective of history, the fact that it has enabled a majority of humanity to become integrated into long-established international structures and to work for their transformation so that, with the inclusion of the Third World, the approach will include every continent and become global, may prove more important than its frequent failures in finding a solution to concrete political issues. Furthermore, it may be well to remember that although the powers have often sought a solution to their problems outside the organization, their daily contacts with the new countries at the

United Nations gave them some understanding of their eventual reactions. In their direct confrontations, the Western and the Communist countries cannot forget that their decisions or lack of agreement, insofar as they affect the world, cannot overlook the views and the reactions of the developing countries.

xi   Closing the Gap

> To make it possible for the Third World to effect
> its integration into the world means to accept the
> integration of the world. The forces set loose by
> the revolution of our time can be diverted only
> at the cost of disaster. They point toward unity and
> co-operation. There is no alternative if humanity
> is to survive.

The Third World was born in the wake of the same transforming forces that catapulted men into space, released the
awesome power of the atom, and brought unprecedented
prosperity to the economically advanced nations. It owes
its birth to the revolution of our time.

This revolution in all its component parts—including the
emergence of the Third World—is leading humanity
toward the realization of its oneness. It does so with inex-
orable evidence. No matter how far away, no matter what
the stage of its development, no country today can escape
the political impact of new discoveries. The nuclear
weapon threatens not only the potential combatants but
humanity as a whole. A small part of the stockpile would
be sufficient to make all life cease on earth. The effects of

nuclear tests upon the present and future generations are broadly the same for the peoples of Asia and the Americas, Africa, and Europe. Space explorations are in their early stages, and we cannot anticipate how deeply they will change the pattern of human relations. Thanks to Telstar a presidential press conference can be viewed simultaneously in every part of the globe. "Spy" satellites can photograph every corner of the earth and reveal jealously guarded military secrets.

The trend toward globalism is becoming evident not only in the interaction of political phenomena, but also in a growing economic interdependence. To an audience of housewives complaining about the fat shortage the late British Foreign Secretary, Ernest Bevin, had this to say: "You complain because you can't get fish suppers in Lancashire. Why can't you get fish suppers? The Fleetwood trawlers are bringing in the fish and there's plenty of potatoes. But the fish-fryers can't fry. And why can't they fry? Because there's trouble in Indonesia; because there's a lot of bother in Burma and because we haven't got things straightened out in Siam. And because of all that, India can't get rice from these countries. And because India has to grow more food for its own people, we can't get ground nuts from India. And because we can't get ground nuts from India, the fish-fryers can't get the oil. And you can't get your fish and chips." [1]

Whenever the impact is global, the solutions must be global, too; they cannot concern one or two continents only but must include all continents and the whole of humanity that lives in them—not only Europe (West and East) and North America, but also Asia, Africa, and Latin America.

The birth of the Third World has made this possible by adding the missing link to a world-wide approach that the scientific revolution makes inescapable.

To say this does not deny the claims of nationalism, but merely reproportions its role. The history of Europe shows that when nationalism operates unassisted in awakening the national consciousness, it faces obstacles such as Africa and Asia have not known, and that are ultimately surmounted after prolonged and bloody struggles. Algeria and Vietnam are the exceptions that prove the rule. Asia and Africa were lifted by the hurricane of irresistible changes that swept over the world with an impact incomparably greater than the wind of nationalism. They are driven to keep pace with transformations that compress in a few years the evolution of centuries. In the process the international balance is being constantly upset, requiring intercontinental efforts to re-establish an equilibrium. Our time is marked by the contradiction between systems corresponding to a reality that already belongs to the past and a new world without a philosophy expressing its newness, or at least an agreed way of establishing priorities of urgency in international relations.

The present transitional nature of the Third World contributes to the contradiction. The emerging continents cannot force on the powers their interpretation of peaceful coexistence. They can only rely upon a "moral force." They have no alternative but to stake their demands in the name of justice, equality, and peace. These are lofty ideals, more easily preached than practiced. An effective participation in global decision-making is dependent upon the consolidation of Afro-Asian independence. The transition to viability requires deep internal changes which can be carried out only if the international balance is modified sufficiently to ensure their realization. The final aim is the recognition of equality.

For the first time in history, the principle of equality—in the sense that all countries have a right to a say in international affairs even though their actual weight in world politics cannot, of course, be the same—is being gradually accepted in the relations among states and applied to weak and unprepared nations. It is implicit in membership in the United Nations and in the efforts by the powers to seek friends where they cannot find allies. This represents a considerable step forward, and is another example of how the Third World carries more weight than its actual strength would justify. The translation of equality into an effective participation in decisions having international repercussions is yet to come. It may be a long time before this tenet that in democratic societies represents the foundation of relations among individuals—irrespective of divisive tendencies such as wealth, race, religion, or national origin—is extended to relations among nations. A different code of international behavior must first be adopted. The Third World believes that only peaceful coexistence offers an international approach to matters which concern humanity as a whole. In a sense, peaceful coexistence is an instrument of globalism, requiring that all nations shift their primary concern from what divides to what unites. Power blocs—military, political, or economic—defeat the purpose of unity. So do totalitarian ideologies and their exploitation for purposes of foreign policy. There cannot be ideological solidarity in the present world, but all countries, irrespective of ideological orientation or form of government, can join without losing their identity in an effort to solve the problems besetting a vast portion of humanity. The nuclear menace in the climate of the cold war is immensely dangerous and the measures required to relieve it have top priority. The menace, however, is man-made, and only the will of men can do away with it. It exists because of disputes among the powers that only they themselves are in a position to regulate. The other countries can intervene and bring pressures to bear, but they are the first to recognize that their role is secondary.

The closing of the gap, on the other hand, is a task of immense complexity, requiring the constant and active cooperation of all continents and countries; all of them share the responsibility. It requires slow and unrelenting work at all levels of international relations—political, economic, psychological. Practically all Third World countries share with United Nations Secretary-General U Thant the conviction that "the present division of the world into rich and poor countries is . . . much more real and much more serious, and ultimately much more explosive, than the division of the world on ideological grounds." [2]

This aspect of the gap is not the outcome of unsurmountable obstacles. It may have appeared inevitable in the past; it no longer is so today. "For the first time in history," U Thant said, "resources are available to match our most imaginative schemes. The truth about the developed economies is that they can have, in terms of kind and scale of resources, what they *decide* to have. Defense spending may consume $120 billion annually, but at the same time the

developed economies have never had higher living standards. . . . And even after all that wealth is poured into armaments, there is still spare labor, idle capacity, a surplus of
food and vast stockpiles of metals. . . . The means are therefore no longer a limiting factor; the will to use our many
and various instruments of change and growth is the only
limitation. It is well within the power of modern man to
eradicate the vast areas of poverty in a world of plenty." [3]

History teaches that every new concept tending to upset
the established order is resisted. It triumphs in the end only
if its drive is greater than the forces opposing it. The Third
World needs a change of direction in international affairs
in order to reach viability; at the same time, until it
achieves viability, it lacks the means to bring enough pressure to bear on the powers to make them change direction.
In order to come out of this vicious circle it must rely upon
outer forces over which it has only a limited measure of
control. Once again, the drive is furnished by the present
revolution. It directs man's mind to universal problems,
thus conditioning it to an understanding of the Third
World's requirement for a global approach.

This work of slow penetration acts during a particularly
difficult period in the process of decolonization. Viability
is a term having a very broad meaning. It envelops the
whole life of a people and cannot be limited purely to
economic conditions. As youth is influenced by its environment, which leaves a lasting imprint on lives, so are the
young nations influenced by the international atmosphere
that the longer-established nations have a primary responsibility in creating. We must remember that the leaders of
the new nations are steered by the experience of other

countries with a profoundly different historical background. Most of these leaders today are the *first* prime ministers or presidents of their respective countries, guided by Western precepts that in the long run may prove inadequate in the Asian and African environment. The obligations of the Third World are great, but those of the other two worlds are much greater. This is especially true of the West because it initiated the vast changes and sparked the ideas now sweeping through the world.

To the extent that the Third World is being pushed forward by forces beyond its control, it cannot keep up with the transformations that the rapid pace produces. The objectives are thus inevitably beyond the immediate capacity of Asia and Africa to realize. This is why the direction taken by the new countries is far more vital than their present attitudes. What counts about India, for example, is that it holds the key to the future of Asia and not so much what stand it takes on Germany or that a certain cabinet minister is ill-tempered. Too often decisions are taken which do not anticipate sweeping transformations in the years to come. The most advanced European nations were at one time a mixture of tribes not far dissimilar from parts of Africa today. Whoever has read the novels of Dickens knows the conditions of unbelievable misery and humiliation in which millions of workmen lived. The rapid transformations caused by industrialization had their frightening side. The changes that the now industrialized countries underwent during recent decades were greater than those of the preceding two thousand years. There is no reason to believe that under the impact of today's revolution the Third World will not also undergo a very rapid evolution. The alternative would be a serious retrogression, a moving backward, with consequences too serious to envisage.

The Third World is being influenced by Western experience, but this does not necessarily mean that it will develop politically into an image of the West. Bridges of understanding will have to be built at levels other than the purely political. "It is evident," economist and historian Walt W. Rostow stated, "that Western political democracy cannot be simply transplanted in societies which have had a different cultural and institutional heritage." But he added: "Deep in the non-Western cultures are moral canons which would assert the integrity of the individual, and which would regard that government as good which, by one route or another, is subject to the consent of the governed." He expressed confidence that "the human values embedded in their cultures will assert themselves and suffuse the life of the modern societies that, in time, they [the non-Western peoples] will surely create." [4] Points of contact with the Third World must be sought particularly at the individual and social levels, because it is these levels and these alone which will determine the political outcome in Asia and Africa.

For these same reasons, the West cannot be deterred in its long-range policies by the lack of confidence often shown by the new countries. Colonialism has done some good, but has also produced deep wounds that only time will heal. Peoples who have been exploited for such a long time cannot be expected to show much gratitude for an economic assistance that they consider to be only a partial restitution for earlier depredations. Nor does it help much to display statistics purporting to prove that the colonial countries have poured more money into the colonies than they have taken away in the form of agricultural products and raw materials. Asia and Africa will keep on believing that Europe grew rich at their expense, and that that is the only reason they are poor. The purpose of assistance is to smooth the difficult transition to viable political structures and to a kind of society that will respect certain fundamental principles. Its final achievement must be to close the gap of understanding, to ensure that, despite their differences, there shall not be between the West and the Third World that wall of suspicion, fear, and profound incompatibility which today exists between the West and the Communist countries.

The West has an interest to proceed in this direction despite attitudes that it may at times consider "provocative." Decolonization, we must remember, is a process of separation from old ties established by the West itself. The charges of neocolonialism will multiply with the difficulties. Third World emotions can be expected to turn increasingly against the West until the bridge can at last be built that will lead to closer links. Americans like to be liked. They may find it particularly hard to accept the mounting criticisms that go hand in hand with insistent requests for more and more assistance. There is already the widespread feeling that the Third World is more anxious to be understood than to understand.

These uncertainties emerge frequently in the press and in Congressional debates. Many people ask: Why should the United States be concerned? The Third World countries are not helping us in our contest with the Soviets,

why should we help them with our money? What difference does it make to us what happens to Asia and Africa,
anyway?

The most compelling reason for caring is that the future
of the United States is irreversibly tied to the future of the
rest of the world, and will be even more so in the years to
come. This country is already under strong Third World
pressure because the new balance that Asia and Africa
insist on seeing established involves all countries, but especially the powers. It involves first of all the United States
and the Soviet Union, two nations without a colonial past
in the traditional sense. In this connection, we must remember that colonialism, as the Third World defines the
term, is whatever stands in the way of the achievement of
peaceful coexistence. The future of coexistence, in turn, is
dependent to a large extent upon the policies of the two
superpowers and the status of their mutual relations. If the
Third World appears always to be picking on the West,
the reason is that decolonization involves the West only,
while peaceful coexistence requires the co-operation of
both the Western and the Communist countries. Decolonization is a process going on now; peaceful coexistence is
an ideal. The West is involved in both; the Soviets only in
the latter. That is why the Third World is twice as bitter
toward the West as toward the Soviet Union. As a leader
in the technological revolution, the United States is largely
if indirectly responsible for the changes that the developing countries are undergoing. As the richest among the rich
countries, it also provokes the strongest reactions on the
part of the proletarian nations. Its economic involvement

in Asia and Africa is today very great. Its responsibilities are as weighty as those of the former colonial countries.

It is not enough to look at these problems with an eye on the situation prevailing today. The West will be soon confronted with the implications of the population explosion. Scientists are convinced that the world can support a population four or more times greater than the present, but this knowledge is of little comfort when one realizes that the four-billion mark will be passed in less than twenty years. A further billion people will be crowding our planet without anything equal to the challenge being done. The time element is of the essence. Unless the developing countries industrialize with reasonable speed and improve the living standards of their citizens, the populations of the emerging countries, Asia in particular, may grow to the point of confronting the industrialized world with the greatest danger in their history.

The resulting pauperization of a majority of humanity would exert the kind of pressure that no diplomatic refinement or balance of power could keep in check. No barriers would be sufficient to contain it, but only the instruments of mass destruction. Population growth is another outcome of the scientific revolution which has reduced infant mortality, increased life expectancy, and practically wiped out epidemics. The new countries cannot industrialize unless their peoples have the energy that an adequate diet can provide. Neither the problem of hunger nor that of increasing the speed of the transition to viability can be handled piecemeal, on an emergency basis, plugging a hole here or there. Only a global attack can solve them, and that requires the kind of world approach the rich countries do not possess in sufficient measure. As Ritchie Calder, Professor of International Relations, Edinburgh University, warned in his forceful book, *Common Sense About a Starving World,* it is likely that in another twenty years "the donors of today will be the suppliants of tomorrow." [5] Unless the Third World's reasonable demands are satisfied, it may one day become a danger to the industrialized countries. Today, it occupies on the international scene a position similar to that of Europe's emerging proletarian class a century or so ago. The West underwent deep changes in order to assimilate the proletariat into the political and social life of the nation. By so doing, it averted the dire consequences that Karl Marx had forecast, leading to the destruction of capitalism and the triumph of communism. Instead, communism triumphed in Russia, where change had been resisted and the claims of the emerging classes ignored. Realism and self-preservation represent, in the final analysis, an awareness of the direction in which the world is moving. Even within the short-range framework of the cold war, the West has an urgent interest in reviewing its relations with the Third World.

The most forceful reason for the United States is furnished by the 1952 report of the President's Policy Commission, presided over by William S. Paley, which assessed the supplies of raw materials necessary to keep this country economically prosperous. In 1950, the United States used 2,700,000,000 tons of raw materials and increased its demand at a rate of 3 per cent yearly. The consumption of petroleum, rubber, iron ore, manganese, and zinc was more than half the world's total supply. The report showed that this country had become dependent for a large percentage of its industrial requirements upon the developing countries. "The over-all objective of a national materials policy for the United States," the Paley report stated, "should be to ensure an adequate and dependable flow of materials at the lowest cost consistent with national security and with the welfare of friendly nations." Thus it was recognized that the self-interest of the United States dictated a policy which would preserve the friendship of the developing nations and ensure their welfare.

These two aims cannot, except on an emergency basis, be attained through handouts. They require the realization that Asia, Africa, and Latin America do not want to be forever continents whose economic structures are entirely geared to exports of materials needed by the industrialized world. A country like Britain, which imports 50 per cent of its food requirements and most of the raw materials for its industry, prospers *also because* the poor countries are getting poorer, and also because it imports from them at lower prices and exports to them at higher prices. To ensure the welfare that will keep their friendship, Britain, like the other industrialized countries, will have to pay more for its imports even if this means a slight lowering in the standard of living, and become adjusted to the idea that, by industrializing, the now poor countries will one day become competitors. The alternative is a situation that could soon get out of control and imperil a vital source of supplies for the industrialized world.

The rich countries today have a much greater flow of trade among themselves than with the poor countries. Europe, not the Third World or Latin America, is the United States' best customer. When the standard of living rises, so do the needs that go with a better life. Paul G. Hoffman, the distinguished American who contributed so greatly to an understanding of the needs of the developing countries, wrote: "If per capita income in the underdeveloped world were lifted by only one percent per year more in the 1960s than they rose in the 1950s, export markets for the entire industrially advanced world would expand by billions of dollars. For the United States—assuming it continues to retain its current share of the international trade flow—such an increase would amount to an estimated additional $7,000,000,000 in United States exports per year by 1970. In man-hours alone an equivalent of more than 4,500,000 jobs in the United States depend on foreign trade. Of these, more than 1,750,000 jobs depend on United States exports to the underdeveloped areas of the world. By 1970 this number may well double to the equivalent of more than 3,500,000 full-time jobs. Assuming a growth of an additional one per cent per year in per capita incomes in the underdeveloped countries, the total exports for this ten-year period as a whole can reasonably be expected to reach $320,000,000,000 from the developed to the underdeveloped world. That is good business. Economic development is not charity; it is sound business management in exactly the same sense that product or market development is sound business management." [6]

The Third World represents a potentially rich market, but it can only import in the measure that it exports. According to the General Agreement on Tariffs and Trade secretariat, the developing countries would have to increase their present trade deficit by $15,000,000,000 by 1975 if they were to achieve an increase of their national income by 5 per cent, which the United Nations General Assembly considered in 1961 a "minimum desirable rate." It is hopeless to expect that governments will increase grants to the extent needed to fill the gap. Public or private loans would in the long run prove too burdensome. The only practical remedy lies in the development of new exports by developing countries and the acceptance of such exports by industrial countries.[7]

No matter how the problem is viewed, the conclusion must always be that there is no solution outside a working arrangement between the developed and the developing countries and the recognition of the political implications of this cooperation. At the present time 85 per cent of the world's wealth is in the hands of 18 per cent of its population. In the 1970's the proportion may be 90 per cent and 8 per cent respectively. This kind of situation cannot lead to anything but disaster. As Barbara Ward so aptly stated, "the need is to remove the work of world development from the subsidiary attention of the wealthy nations and to make it a central theme of their diplomacy, their international relations, their philosophy of world order, their hopes for a future in which not only groups and nations but the human race itself can hope to make this small planet into a habitable home." [8]

As supplier of raw materials the Third World contributes to the preservation of the military posture of the United States. At the moment, most of the countries of Africa and Asia are unaligned and in a few instances are allied to the West. This helps to preserve the continental character of the Communist World which represents a huge mass of contiguous countries.

The West, on the other hand, is primarily maritime in nature. The groups of countries composing it are separated by oceans and the raw materials needed for their industries must move by sea. The Third World plays an important role in the control of the seas not only because many Asian and African countries have long coasts, but also because they block Soviet access to the oceans. Even though China has furnished the Communist world with a seacoast of nearly two thousand miles, access to the Pacific Ocean proper is guarded by a chain of islands that from Japan to the Philippines are allied to the West and beyond are unaligned. The last war has also shown the importance that West Africa acquires for moving sea traffic from its ports to Brazil and North America. Equally important are the Suez Canal and the Red Sea routes which are almost entirely controlled by Third World countries.[9]

To believe that the raw materials and the unhampered control of the sea routes will always be available to the West means to take the Third World for granted. The West may find that this is the worst possible policy to follow with regard to Asia and Africa. The day will inevitably come when the two continents will exact a price that cannot be paid in money only. What they want, and what they must have, is the fundamental change of policy that has been described in the preceding pages. Their means of pressure will increase with their development. One day they may not have to rely so heavily upon outer forces or on the need to play one power bloc against the other. They will possess, sooner or later, the inner strength they now lack. The West can only hope that this day will come as soon as possible because the alternative would be an interminable series of crises far more difficult to handle and presenting an even greater peril.

Because the Third World is proletarian it can only negotiate a solution with all the rich countries. It will keep insisting, therefore, that the rich countries settle their own problems first. This is the essence of nonalignment. It would be unrealistic to expect the Third World to deviate from this policy because its future depends upon the establishment of relations that are not overwhelmingly dominated by the competition between the West and the Communist countries. To respect this position and to understand its implications is the only constructive policy for the West. As the developing continents proceed along the road to viability, they will move gradually away from the West and the type of ties established by colonialism. A new relationship will then have to be negotiated among equals. This is the best outcome the West can hope for. Should the revolutionary forces that are driving the Third World toward modernization prove ineffective, the outcome would be total chaos, marked by one explosive outbreak after the other.

To make it possible for the Third World to effect its integration into the world means to accept the integration of the world. The forces set loose by the revolution of our time can be diverted only at the cost of disaster. They point toward unity and cooperation. There is no alternative if humanity is to survive.

Notes

Notes

I. Introduction

1. We prefer to use the word "developing" rather than "underdeveloped" or "less developed" because it reflects more clearly the Third World's efforts to overcome its present economic inferiority compared to the developed countries. Development is, of course, relative. For example, Spain is a developed country compared with the Congo but an underdeveloped one compared with the United States. The United States, in turn, is more developed today than it was only a few decades ago and will be still more developed in a few decades than it is today. In this respect, practically every country is "developing." This terminology refers exclusively to economic, and not to cultural or intellectual, conditions.

II. World-Wide Revolution

1. A. J. P. Taylor, *The Struggle for Mastery in Europe* (Oxford: Clarendon Press, 1954), p. 568.
2. Rupert Emerson, *From Empire to Nation* (Cambridge: Harvard University Press, 1960), p. 45.
3. Quoted by Lester B. Pearson in his Nobel Peace Prize Lecture, December 11, 1957.

III. The Gap

1. Christopher Dawson, *The Making of Europe* (New York: Meridian Books, 1958), p. 243.
2. Barbara Ward, *The Rich Nations and the Poor Nations* (New York: W. W. Norton, 1962), pp. 17-18.
3. *Ibid.*, p. 20.
4. *Ibid.*, pp. 45-46.
5. The earth's population, which in 1860 was 1,250 million, doubled in less than a century. It is anticipated that another 1,250 million will be added in the twenty-five-year period from 1950 to 1975. From 1975 to 2000, the further increase will probably be of 2,500 million or more. "It is difficult to imagine the conditions in a world inhabited by more than double the number of people now in existence. And it is most debatable whether the trends in mortality and fertility can continue much longer with the degree of inertia which has characterized them in the past. Factors other than the slow secular changes in fertility and mortality may eventually bring population growth to a halt. Otherwise, even if it is conceded that population growth, after its peak near the end of our century, might diminish gradually and cease within another century, world population would not stop growing until it had reached between 10,000 and 25,000 million. One cannot say that such further growth is utterly impossible, but the vast changes in human organization required to sustain it can hardly be conceived at the present time." United Nations ST/SOA/Series A/28, *The Future Growth of World Population,* (Population Studies, No. 28, 1958), p. 21.
6. "More than half the world's people live in Asia and the proportion is likely to surpass three-fifths before the century is ended. There will be a continued decline in the relative importance of Europe, including

the Soviet Union. Early in this century, there was an European for every two Asians; by the end of the century, this ratio may have become 1 to 4." *Ibid.,* p. 24.

7. In North America, food production is 60 per cent higher than it was before World War II while the population has increased by only 33 per cent. In Asia, the increase was by about 28 per cent while population has gone up by about 33 per cent.

8. *The United Nations Development Decade* (United Nations: Department of Economic and Social Affairs, 1962), p. 5.

9. These proportions vary according to the methods employed to compute them. Based on exchange rates, the percentages for the developed and the developing parts of the world, but excluding the Communist countries, is 78.5 and 21.5, respectively. Based on the buying power of the national monies, the percentage becomes 69.9 and 30.1, and the index of per capita income (per capita income in the world = 100) 269 and 41. J. P. Delahaut and E. S. Kirschen, "Les revenus nationaux du monde non-communiste," *Cahiers Économiques de Bruxelles,* No. 10, (April, 1961), *passim.*

Statistical measurements are notoriously inadequate when dealing with poor countries. More food is bought with one dollar in Ceylon than in the United States and the need for clothing and housing is less in warm countries than in those situated in the colder zone. The fact remains, however, that during the 1950-59 decade the net increase in income per person in the developing countries was terribly low. According to Paul G. Hoffman, the estimated annual rate of increase was 3 per cent. But considering that the population increased by 2 per cent, all that the average man got in ten years was ten dollars more, or one dollar per year. During the same period, per capita income, in dollars of constant purchasing power, increased by 225 dollars in the United States and by over 200 dollars in the six countries of the European Economic Community. Real per capita income has been rising in the industrialized countries at the rate of about 2½ per cent during the 1950's, and in the less developed countries at a rate of about 1 per cent. "Obviously, then, the income gap is widening." Paul G. Hoffman, *One Hundred Countries One and One-quarter Billion People* (Washington, D.C.: Albert D. and Mary Lasker Foundation, 1960), p. 22.

10. "Major cities in these areas have large hovel settlements in which as much as 20 or 30 per cent of a city's population may live in rudimentary shelters, with no water, sewers, roads, or other community facilities. Rural areas are even more deficient in the basic services and the facilities necessary for healthy rural communities which can reduce migration to urban areas. In cities and rural areas alike, conditions are aggravated by unduly high rents which critically reduce expenditures on food or clothing, and by insecurity of tenure. Dissatisfaction with housing and living conditions leads to political and social instability and tensions. In virtually all developing countries housing conditions are deteriorating steadily, despite the fact that these countries are allocating to housing a share of gross domestic fixed investment ranging from 12 per cent to as high as 30 per cent." To make matters worse, it is estimated that over 200 million new inhabitants will crowd into the cities of Africa, Asia, and Latin America during the next ten years. *The United Nations Development Decade*, p. 25.

11. About 1957 or 1958, the number of people per doctor

numbered 900 or less in such countries as Austria, Belgium, Italy, the Netherlands, New Zealand, Spain, the United States, and the USSR, but more than 20,-000 to each doctor in Ghana, Laos, Madagascar, New Guinea, and Sierra Leone and more than 40,000 per doctor in Afghanistan, the French-speaking countries of West Africa, Nigeria, Sudan, and Togoland.

12. In this field, too, the differences between industrialized and developing countries are marked. In the U.S. and USSR together, there are twice as many young men and women enrolled in institutions of higher education than in the whole of Africa, Asia, and Latin America. According to UNESCO estimates, in tropical Africa 17,000,000 children are without classroom space; between 80 and 85 per cent of the adult population is illiterate; fewer than 5 per cent of the children who do attend a primary school go on to secondary school; fewer than 1 per cent of those attending school are enrolled in vocational training institutes. During the decade 1950-60, the illiteracy rate has increased significantly in certain heavily populated countries, notably in Asia.

13. Germaine Tillion, *Algeria* (New York: Alfred A. Knopf, 1958), p. 28.

14. Pierre Moussa, *Les Nations Prolétaires* (Paris: Presses Universitaires de France, 1959), p. 5.

IV. Peaceful Coexistence

1. Mamadou Dia, *The African Nations and World Solidarity* (New York: Frederick A. Praeger, 1961), p. 13.

2. Jawaharlal Nehru, *Glimpses of World History* (New York: John Day Company, 1942), p. 182.

V. Anticolonialism

1. From an address before the Academic Association of the University of Lund, Lund, Sweden, May 4, 1959.

Reprint from *United Nations Review,* Vol. VI, No. 1 (July, 1959), p. 3.

2. Michael Edwardes, *Asia in the Balance* (Baltimore, Maryland: Penguin Books, 1962), p. 188.

3. Rupert Emerson, *From Empire to Nation,* pp. 278-79.

4. Quoted in Jean Lacouture and Jean Baumier, *Le Poids du Tiers Monde* (Paris: Arthaud, 1962), p. 197: "Le Socialisme se définit pour nous comme la méthode qui met la recherche et les techniques— politiques, économiques, sociales et culturelles—au service de la socialisation 'panhumaine': de la civilisation de l'universel. C'est l'humanisme des temps contemporains. La négritude, de négative, se fait positive. Elle reste l'ensemble des valeurs—politiques, morales, sociales, culturelles—du monde noir. Mais elle est désormais fondée non sur une seule race, mais encore sur la géographie et l'histoire—histoire politique et économique. Ce sont les valeurs culturelles du coeur qui constitueront les apports des nègres nouveaux 'au rendez-vous du donner et du recevoir' au courant convergent de socialisation, pour tout dire au *socialisme rectifié.*"

5. Ahmed ben Salah, "Significations et perspectives de la décolonisation," *Esprit,* Vol. XXV, No. 251 (June, 1957), p. 891: "Sous peine de conduire à une marche à rebours, à une régression, la décolonisation ne doit pas être le processus inverse de la colonisation. L'échec de plusieurs pays anciennement colonisés ne s'explique que par ce formalisme superficiel, négatif et stérile. La décolonisation doit d'abord signifier une révolution profonde des structures mentales, morales, sociales et économiques. Cette révolution n'est pas destruction de l'acquit colonial, mais utilisation et réorientation fondamentales de cet acquit consideré comme un instrument arraché à la colonisation et susceptible de recevoir une nouvelle destination."

6. W. R. Crocker, *Self-Government for the Colonies* (London: George Allen & Unwin, Ltd., 1949), p. 8.
7. Vera Micheles Dean, "Democracy East and West," *The Progressive,* Vol. XXVI, No. 7 (July, 1962), p. 18.
8. As late as 1871, Africa was still largely unexplored. European penetration reached only the coastal areas of Algeria, South Africa, and a few trading points along the Atlantic coast. After the Congress of Berlin of 1878, a new European expansion began, and before the end of the century the partition of Africa was practically completed. Europe's control of the continent lasted, therefore, less than three-quarters of a century. In Asia, except for the Spanish Philippines which were fully conquered before the end of the seventeenth century, European powers established their colonial rule during the second half of the nineteenth century. Britain's presence in India dates back to the seventeenth century, but the colonial administration proper can be said to have begun in 1858, when the British Crown took over the administration from the British East India Company. Burma was completely occupied in 1886. The consolidation of Dutch rule over Indonesia occurred shortly before World War I. In Indo-China effective French rule dates from the end of the nineteenth century.
9. See Chapter VIII.

VI. Nonalignment

1. U.N. Doc. E/3593 (February 28, 1962), p. 10.
2. *Ibid.,* p. 73.
3. *The United Nations Development Decade,* p. 8.
4. *Ibid.,* p. 12-13.
5. *Economic and Social Consequences of Disarmament,* p. 72.
6. "L'esquisse de notre position se situera, selon les

problèmes, près d'un bloc ou loin d'un autre, avec un bloc ou avec l'autre et, le cas échéant, les rapprochera. Notre boussole? La paix, la justice et la liberté. Notre attitude se définit uniquement en fonction des objectifs que nous nous sommes fixés. Assurément une telle définition du non-alignement est à la fois sommaire et banale, mais elle limite et simplifie les termes du problème et en précise le contenu."

vii. Cold War

1. The New York *Herald Tribune,* November 30, 1961.

viii. The Third World and the West

1. Janez Stanovnik, "The Cairo Declaration and International Economic Relations," *Borba* (Belgrade, Yugoslavia), August 19, 1962.

2. From 38 per cent after World War II, it fell to 36 per cent in 1953, to 31 per cent in 1959, and to 29 per cent in 1961.

3. From an address to the Bari Symposium of the EEC Commission, October 7-8, 1961.

4. United Nations E/ECE/419, *Economic Survey of Europe in 1960* (Prepared by the Secretariat of the Economic Commission for Europe, Geneva: 1961), Ch. V, p. 49.

5. From a statement by Philippe de Seynes, Under-Secretary for Economic and Social Affairs, before a committee of the UN General Assembly (September 26, 1962).

6. Barbara Ward, "Free Africa and the Common Market," *Foreign Affairs,* Vol. 40, No. 3 (April, 1962), p. 420.

7. Moussa, *Les Nations Prolétaires,* pp. 38-39.

8. From an advertisement entitled "Nigeria 1961" in The New York *Herald Tribune,* October 29, 1961.

9. It also happens that countries least willing to break

away from traditional social and economic patterns and averse to modernization are also very loud in their denunciations of "Western imperialism." The speeches by the delegates of Saudi Arabia and Yemen in the UN General Assembly offer edifying examples.
10. Arnold Toynbee, *The World and the West* (New York and London: Oxford University Press, 1952), pp. 2-3.

IX. The Third World and the Communist Countries
1. Owen Lattimore, *The Situation in Asia* (Boston: Little, Brown and Company, 1949), pp. 16-17.
2. "Regional Economic Policy in the Soviet Union: The Case of Central Asia," *Economic Bulletin for Europe*, prepared by the Research and Planning Division, United Nations Economic Commission for Europe, Geneva, Vol. IX, No. 3 (November, 1957), p. 55.
3. *Ibid.,* p. 68.
4. *Ibid.,* p. 73.
5. *Ibid.,* p. 75.

X. United Nations
1. Cyprus also belongs to the group, bringing the total to 55.
2. Francis O. Wilcox, *UN and the Nonaligned Nations* (New York: Foreign Policy Association, Headline Series No. 155, 1962), p. 15.
3. *Ibid.,* p. 16.
4. U.N. Doc. ST/DPI/ SER/A/73, 6 January 1953, *Non-Self-Governing Territories* (Background Paper No. 73), pp. 3-4.
5. United Nations, *Introduction to the Annual Report of the Secretary-General on the Work of the Organization. 16 June 1959-15 June 1960,* p. 2.

XI. Closing the Gap
1. Quoted in Ritchie Calder, *Common Sense About a*

Starving World (New York: The Macmillan Company, 1962), pp. 11-12.

2. United Nations, *Introduction to the Annual Report of the Secretary-General on the Work of the Organization. 16 June 1961-15 June 1962,* p. 3.

3. From an address at University of São Paulo, Brazil, on August 8, 1962 (U.N. Doc. SG/1282), pp. 7-8.

4. From an address September 6, 1962, to the Fifth World Congress of Sociology held in Washington, D.C. (as reported in The New York *Times,* September 7, 1962).

5. Ritchie Calder, *Common Sense About a Starving World,* p. 169.

6. Paul G. Hoffman, "Bread upon the Waters: the Problems and Promises of Development," in *Britannica Book of the Year* (Chicago: Encyclopaedia Britannica, Inc., 1962), p. 8.

7. Jean Royer, "World Trade; the Dangers of Regionalism," *Lloyds Bank Review,* No. 66 (October, 1962), p. 20.

8. "New Perspectives in Economic Development," background paper, Oxford Conference on Tensions in Development, p. 8.

9. Moussa, *Les Nations Prolétaires,* pp. 172-74.

Index

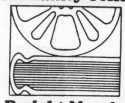